THE ESSEX COUNTY COUNCIL, CHELMSFORD
ESSEX RECORD OFFICE PUBLICATIONS, No. 55
1970

Printed by
CULLINGFORD & CO. LTD., COLCHESTER

———

EIGHT SHILLINGS AND

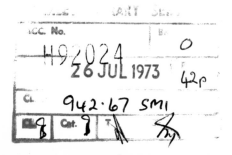

CONTENTS

PREFACE

The idea of writing this book stemmed from research undertaken in the late summer and autumn of 1969 for an exhibition on the history of Foulness to be mounted at the Essex Record Office exhibition centre at Ingatestone Hall the following spring. It very soon became apparent that there was sufficient documentary and good secondary material available to form the basis of a book, and the Library and Records Committee of the Essex County Council readily agreed to include it in the Essex Record Office series of publications.

Although this book is a study in some detail of one Essex island and marshland parish, parallels with other similar Essex parishes have been drawn where appropriate, and in many spheres, particularly those of medieval economy and the pre-Domesday sub-division of the island between several mainland manors, Foulness is typical of the region. But in at least one important aspect it is probably unique, for nowhere in the county has an example yet been found of such early land reclamation ('inning') from the sea, which at Foulness began before about 1420.

Mention is made in Chapter VIII of the possibility that the third London airport and a great dock complex will be constructed on the Maplin and Foulness Sands, but no attempt is made to assess the merits and disadvantages of this. It is incidental therefore, that this study appears at the beginning of an era which might, within the space of a few years, result in more fundamental economic and environmental changes than have occurred over the last millenium.

ACKNOWLEDGEMENTS

This book, like any work based on research, incorporates much learning of other scholars available in print and typescript, and my debt to them is, I hope, fully acknowledged in the footnotes. I am particularly indebted to Mr. K. C. Newton, M.A., F.R.Hist.S., the County Archivist of Essex, for much advice and guidance, especially with Chapter II, where his medieval expertise has proved invaluable. The researches of Miss H. E. P. Grieve, B.E.M., B.A., for *The Great Tide* (1959) have saved me long hours of hard work, and much of her original work is incorporated in Chapters I, II, V and VI. For help with the necessary field-work on the island I am grateful to Mr. and Mrs. P. A. Arnold of Lodge Farm and Mr. Peter Lilley of Courtsend. Mr. Arnold has also freely made available his excellent statistics on the island, in particular those on present day population and farming. Mr. J. M. L. Booker, B.A., Senior Assistant Archivist, has read the text and corrected my more unorthodox grammar. Mr. R. Bates and Mr. D. Tobias of the County Visual and Aural Aids Service have bestowed their customary skill and care on producing the photographs for illustrations 1, 3–8, which form part of a photographic survey of the island conducted in August 1969, and which, because cameras are not normally allowed on the island, was carried out by kind permission of the Commandant, Proof and Experimental Establishment, Shoeburyness.

J. R. SMITH

CHAPTER I

GEOLOGY AND ARCHAEOLOGY[1]

Britain forms part of the Continental land mass and a million or more years ago man and beast could pass on foot between Britain and the Continent by a low-lying land bridge. At its maximum extent this land bridge afforded relatively dry access from the Danish coast to eastern England, while the southern limit of the North Sea followed a line extending from the north Lincolnshire coast to just north of Jutland. The Thames, following a more northerly course, was a tributary of a great northward flowing river, probably the old course of the Rhine.

About 600,000 B.C. began the first of four great periods of glaciation (the four Ice Ages), with three warmer intervals. The ice sheet attained its greatest extent in the penultimate glaciation, roughly 230,000–187,000 B.C., when it reached as far south as Finchley in Middlesex and the northern parts of Hertfordshire and Essex. The final retreat began about 20,000 B.C. and as the ice melted the sea slowly rose from a level rather more than 300 feet below the present mean level of tides and the more northerly land, relieved of the enormous weight of ice, rose, even relative to the rising sea level. This process is continuing and may be seen in the 'raised beaches' of north-west Scotland and from the position of the mooring rings of medieval Baltic harbours now no longer navigable by so much as a rowing boat. But while the north has risen, the land of south-east England and the Netherlands has sunk relative to the sea, and is still sinking, at a rate of six to twelve inches a century on the Essex coast.

The 'official' ending of the Ice Age is normally taken as 7912 B.C., when the ice withdrew from the central Swedish moraine, but the melting process is still continuing in the great polar regions, and it has been estimated that if the ice masses of those regions were to melt, and their stored water returned to the oceans, the sea level would rise some 200 feet, with devastating results.

As the ice sheets melted and the sea level rose, the land bridge between Britain and the Continent gradually became submerged, until sometime in the millenium 7000 to 6000 B.C., or perhaps even later, the North Sea finally cut through the Straits of Dover, and Britain became an island. There had been earlier separations during the three main warm periods between the four glaciations, and it is conceivable that at some time in the future Britain will again become joined to the Continent.

In the Essex marshlands alternating layers of silt (mud deposited by water) and peat (vegetation decomposed by water) stand as evidence of the sea's periods of advance and retreat. Preserved in these layers is archaeological evidence which shows that the sea has engulfed areas where people once lived. For example, at Great Clacton and at Lion Point, Jaywick, evidence has come to light of one of the early flake-using[2] peoples, known as Clactonian after the site where they were first recognised. They date from the first inter-glacial period (c.525,000–475,000 B.C.) and the Clacton site was on the shore of the ancient course of the Thames.

There is also a wealth of Roman and Romano-British remains all round the Essex coast. At West Tilbury a Romano-British hut circle is buried on the Thames foreshore about 13 feet below high water mark, and on Canvey Island Romano-British domestic fire-hearths, which 1,900 years ago must have been 4 or 5 feet above high water mark, have been found at depths now 12 to 13 feet below that level. The Roman fort at Bradwell-juxta-Mare, probably 'Othona' (*Ithancester*), one of the series of forts built to defend the 'Saxon Shore' against piratical attacks by Germanic tribes, the ancestors of the East Saxons, is today largely lost under saltings washed by most spring tides. Indeed, the Thames itself is now tidal to Teddington, whereas it appears then to have been tidal no further than London Bridge, which probably accounts for the choice of London as the site for the Roman Capital.

Foulness itself has yielded rich evidence of Romano–British settlement. In 1848 Stephen Allen of Rayleigh Lodge, and the owner of considerable land on the island, levelled a 'barrow' (probably a 'Red Hill') on Loading Marsh, Little Shelford, and found in its centre a large urn and seven or eight other pots round it, of dates from the 2nd to 4th centuries A.D., and of which two are apparently Samian.[3] Philip Benton states that the find had been made 'in a Red Hill between the house and wall'.[4] This group is now in Prittlewell Priory Museum, Southend-on-Sea, where it is preserved together with an archer's wrist guard made of ivory, also Roman, and which is alleged to have been found on Foulness. Red Hills, so called because they are formed of red burnt clay and pottery fragments, are to be found all round the Essex coast. Although some archaeological disagreement still continues, they almost certainly mark the sites of Iron Age and Roman salt works.[5] At the time of Domesday there were 47 salt-pans in the county and the most common sites were in the marshes near tidal inlets,[6] where the water is more saline. Other mounds occurred on the island at Rugwood and Great Burwood,[7] but have been destroyed, apparently without being investigated. W. H. Dalton recorded the existence of three sites during geological examination in 1874,[8] but these, too, are lost.

During this period (2nd–4th centuries A.D.) it is unlikely that there was any need to embank the island against the sea. Indeed, it has been suggested that Foulness was originally not an island at all but formed part of the mainland, and that Shelford and the other creeks which surround the six islands (New England, Foulness, Havengore, Potton, Rushley and Wallasea) that make up the 'Essex Archipelago', are of more recent origin, being formed by the sinking of the land relative to sea level. There is undoubtedly some truth in this suggestion, but the question remains, *when* did the south-east corner of Essex split into six islands? The site of the 'Red Hill' next to Shelford Creek and Edgar Brown's argument that the Broomway is of Roman origin strongly indicate that Foulness, at least, was already an island in Roman times.[9]

The name Foulness means 'the promontory of wild birds', and derives from the Old English *fugla-naess*, or 'wild-birds' ness'. The element 'nase', 'nass' or 'ness' is common in English place-names and refers to a promontory, and apart from Foulness, some of the best examples of use of the element are Skegness (Lincs.), Walton-on-the-Naze (Essex) and Dungeness (Kent).[10]

CHAPTER II

THE MANOR, AGRICULTURE AND FISHING, DOMESDAY TO REFORMATION

Until the mid-16th century, when the island became a separate ecclesiastical parish, Foulness was shared by the mainland parishes of Sutton, Rochford, Shopland, Little Stambridge and Little Wakering, all in Rochford Hundred.[1] Neighbouring Wallasea Island was also originally in five mainland parishes, Canewdon, Great Stambridge, Paglesham, Little Wakering and Eastwood,[2] while Canvey Island was shared by nine parishes.[3] Such was the value attached to the coastal marshlands for grazing, that shares in them were eagerly sought by powerful mainland landowners at an early date. These divisions are pre-Domesday and are the reason why Foulness and many other areas of coastal marshland are not mentioned by name in the Great Survey 1086. In the Essex section of the Little Domesday Book the word 'marsh' occurs only five times, four of which clearly refer to marsh alongside fresh-water streams. For coastal manors, where mention of marshland would be expected, there is entered instead the phrase 'pasture for [so many] sheep', a phrase never used for inland manors, except for those known later to have held 'detached' rights of common of pasture, such as Sutton and Rochford held on Foulness. The value of the marshlands for pasture is further emphasised by the fact that they were divided among *so many* mainland manors and parishes. Canvey, Foulness and Wallasea islands were together shared by no less than eighteen parishes, several being a considerable distance from their detached rights of pasture. According to the Survey, the carrying capacity of the Essex coastal marshlands was in excess of 18,000 sheep.[4]

Mention is first made of the manor of 'Fulness' in 1235,[5] but the two earliest extant records of the manor are bailiffs' account rolls of *c*.1420 and 1424.[6] From these two documents it would seem that the area of the manor was limited to the marshes of South Wick (Foulness Hall Marsh, 525 acres), Nase Wick (366 acres) East Wick (254 acres), Monkton Barns (163 acres) and New Wick (220 acres) which had been 'inned' some time before about 1420.[7] The marsh of Rugwood appears to have been incorporated into the manor for administrative purposes sometime between 1483 and 1486,[8] and Arundel Marsh, which was 'inned' between 1424 and 1486, was also included in the manor.[9]

The area of the manor was thus limited to the eastern (and most valuable) end of the island within the detached parts of Sutton and Rochford,[10] the lordships of which were held at the time of Domesday by the Saxon Suene of Essex, and it may have been that he or his successors created the manor a separate entity as a matter of administrative convenience during the period 1086 and the early 13th century. Suene's vast estates in Essex were forfeited to the Crown by his grandson, and Foulness was subsequently granted to Hubert de Burgh,[11] Earl of Kent and Chief Justiciar, who died in May 1243 and was succeeded by his elder son John.[12] In 1271

> John de Burgo the elder son and heir of Hubert de Burgo late earl of Kent granted to Sir Guy de Rocheford, knight, lord of Rocheford . . . for 700 marks . . . all the donor's marshes, saving to the donor and his heirs the granting (*collatione*) of the tithes of the marshes of Fughelnes in Rochford Hundred . . . within or without the walls (*wallas*) . . .[13]

Guy de Rochford died in 1274, and was succeeded by his nephew John de Rochford.[14] The King had intervened at Guy's death to grant a moiety (half share) of the estates to his widow Margery for the term of her life, and a moiety of the arable of Foulness was said to be worth £13 1s. 8d. yearly and the pasture £6 0s. 4d. yearly.[15] John died in 1309 and the estate passed to his son Robert, aged 30 years.[16] Robert still owned the marshes of Foulness in 1324,[17] but no mention can be found of him in this context after that date. It would appear indeed that shortly afterwards the manor of Foulness was acquired by William de Bohun, Earl of Hereford and Lord High Constable of England.[18] By the fourteenth century the de Bohun family had established a powerful complex of estates in Essex owning 51 manors in the county, and there is evidence to show that Foulness was economically inter-related with the other de Bohun estates at this period.[19]

Humphrey, the last of the de Bohuns, Earl of Hereford, Essex and North-ampton and Lord High Constable of England, died in January 1373 and his co-heirs were his daughters Eleanor, aged 7, and Mary aged 3 or 4.[20] Although Eleanor's portion included the manor of Foulness[21] it was subject to the dower assigned to the widowed Countess Joan who is mentioned as Lady of the Manor in 1386 and 1407.[22] Both Eleanor and Mary died before 1400,[23] thus predeceasing their mother Joan who died in 1419.[24] In 1424 the manor was in the hands of Joan's executors[25] but the ownership for the next 23 years after this date is obscure. In June 1447 it was purchased from Henry VI by James Butler, 5th Earl of Ormond,[26] a zealous Lancastrian, who held it until he was executed at Newcastle in May 1461 following his capture at the battle of Towton (Yorks.) in March.[27] His brothers John and Thomas Butler were attainted[28] and the estates which John (the elder brother) should have inherited were confiscated by the Crown and in 1465 the manor of Foulness was granted to Anne, sister of Edward IV,[29] from whom it passed in 1473 to Thomas Grey (Edward IV's stepson), first Marquis of Dorset, who had married Anne, daughter of Edward IV's sister Anne.[30] In January 1483 it was granted to Lord Richard Grey[31] (Thomas's younger brother) who was beheaded later in the year after having been accused by Richard, Duke of Gloucester, of estranging Edward V from him, and the manor passed once more to the Crown.[32]

In April 1485 Thomas Butler, 7th Earl of Ormond, was granted by Richard III the estates in Essex which had been confiscated in 1461, including the manor of Foulness.[33] It remained in the Butler family until 1527 when Piers Butler, 8th Earl of Ormond, at the special request of Henry VIII surrendered the Ormond title and part of the estate, including Foulness, to Sir Thomas Boleyn, a favourite of the King, created Viscount Rochford in 1525, and whose daughter Anne was to become Queen in 1533.[34] On the death of Thomas Boleyn in 1539[35] the manor of Foulness and the other estates apparently passed to his younger daughter Mary (Anne having been beheaded in 1536) whose first husband William Carey died of 'the sweating sickness' in 1528.[36] Their son Henry Carey, 1st Lord Hunsdon, cousin and lifelong favourite of Queen Elizabeth, sold the manor of Foulness to Sir Richard Rich, Lord Chancellor of England, in November 1549.[37]

Throughout the Middle Ages the Essex marshland sheep were especially prized as a source of dairy produce – milk, butter and particularly cheeses made from ewes' milk. For example, in 1201 Thomas de Camville, Lord of Fobbing, claimed against Robert de Sutton by civil plea, the marsh of Richersness (Russellhead on Canvey Island), alleging that in the time of Henry II (1155–89) his grandfather had taken the profits of it, arising from 'cheeses, wool and rushes'.[38]

A single bailiff's account of the manor of Writtle, 1360–61,[39] shows how one element of the economy of Foulness was inter-related with the other de Bohun manors, for in that year the bailiff of Writtle accounted for 140 new-born lambs received from the neighbouring manor of [Great] Waltham, 80 year-old lambs received from the sub-manor of 'le Roos' in Saffron Walden, 39 'gimmers' (a virgin ewe one year old) sent to Great Waltham and 110 year-old lambs and 8 'multoni' (male sheep kept for wool, meat and skins only) sent to Foulness Island. Shortly after the date of this account the demesne lands at Writtle were leased to tenants of the manor[40] and to discover whether Foulness continued to receive sheep from other inland manors of the de Bohun family would require an examination of the bailiff's accounts for those manors, a task of considerable magnitude.

Sheep's milk was only available in summer time. It was commonly believed that if milking extended into the autumn the animals would have difficulty in mating, and Thomas Tusser, in his *Five Hundred Points of Husbandry* (1573), reckoned

> At Philip and Jacob, away with the lambs,
> That thinkest to have any milke of their dams,
> At Lammas leave milking, for feare of a thing,
> Least *Requiem æternam* in winter they sing.

In 1424 the bailiff of the manor of Foulness, William Daunger, accounted under the heading of 'Dairy' for

> £32 19s. 6d. from rent of milk of 1,319 mother ewes at 6d. per head and not for more because of the sickness of the same, of which 36 are in Southwyk, 50 in Nassewyk, 17 in Estwyck and 15 in Newyk.

He also answered for a total of 1,602 ewes, including 167 taken in from the 'gimmers', during the time of the account (Easter–Michaelmas, 1424). Of these 501 were in South Wick, 498 in Nase Wick, 270 in East Wick and 333 in New Wick. Seventeen, however, died of 'murrain'[41] (7 in South Wick, 6 in Nase Wick, 1 in East Wick and 3 in New Wick), and 109 worn-out ewes (*ouib[us] matric[ibus] cron[atis]*) had been sold by 'Darcy' the steward for £4 3s. 4d. thus leaving at Michaelmas 1,476 ewes (457 in South Wick, 457 in Nase Wick, 250 in East Wick and 312 in New Wick).

Also during the period of the account the bailiff was responsible for 92 rams within the manor of which 16 had grown up from 'young rams', but 4 died of 'murrain' and 6 worn-out rams were sold for 1s. each, leaving 82 at Michaelmas (23 in South Wick, 20 in Nase Wick, 10 in East Wick, 15 in New Wick, and 14 in Monkton Barns). In addition, he accounted for 17 young male lambs (under one year), not castrated (5 in South Wick, 5 in Nase Wick, 3 in East Wick, and 4 in New Wick) at Michaelmas. 400 new-born lambs (presumably born in the spring of 1424) were also accounted for, and of these 397 were sold by 'Darcy' the steward in September for £22 8s. 5d., 2 died and the bailiff had to pay 1s. for one because it was missing from the flock.

The several mentions of 'murrain' above require some explanation. It was 'plague' and the common medieval word for disease in sheep and cattle. Sheep dying of this malady, which was apparently fatal, were not a total loss, for there was a ready market for their wool and skins, and their meat was salted down and preserved.[42]

It has been shown that in 1424 of a total of 1,437 milk-producing ewes within the manor 118 were sick. Although the sickness is not specified it was probably caused by the wetness of the ground, and it is known that precautions were taken to protect the sheep against hoof-rot. In his account of c.1420 the bailiff records the purchase of 2 barrels of tar and 1 barrel of butter 'for sheep's medicine'. The two ingredients were mixed to a paste and coated on the hoofs of sheep as a barrier ointment against the wet. Tar was also applied to cuts and wounds, for example, those caused through bad shearing and marking.

Apart from the manor, there were also a number of other enclosed marshes on the island,[43] and there can be little doubt that they, too, supported large

11

numbers of sheep. In 1594 John Norden described the Hundred of Rochford, in which Foulness lay, as yielding:

> Milke, butter and cheese in admirable abundance, and in these parts are the great and huge cheeses made, wondered at for their massiveness and thickness.[44]

The making of these 'great and huge cheeses' was a profitable occupation. As early as 1173 fifty *magni casei* were bought for Berkhampstead Castle at a cost of 25s., or sixpence each, while 200 ordinary cheeses which were sent to Gloucester cost only £1 13s. 4d., or twopence each.[45] The value of cheese as a food was fully recognised, especially by the peasantry, and the quantities consumed throughout the country were considerable.

Under the section dealing with debts the bailiff of Foulness accounted in Michaelmas 1424 as follows

> John Crank of Maldon for the price of 60 weys of cheese sold to the same by Robert Dracy [Darcy] steward of the court there, at 11s. per wey whereof of the charge of William Carter' shepherd of Southwyk £11 of the charge of John Rede shepherd of Nassewyk £9 7s. of the charge of Richard Duryvall shepherd of Estwyk £6 12s. and of the charge of William Hammond shepherd of Newyk £6 12d.

Thus income in 1424 from 60 weys of cheese at 11s. each amounted to £33 A wey of cheese was stated in the accounts of the officers of St Osyth's Priory (Essex) in 1512 to be 336 pounds, when each 'weighz' sold for 10s.[46] Of the primitive dairies on the Essex coastal marshlands the memory is still preserved in the suffix 'wick', the medieval word for dairy farm. On Foulness three, East Wick, Nase Wick and New Wick, are remembered.[47]

Although dairy produce was the most important, it was by no means the only product of the large flocks of marshland sheep. They were highly valued also for their meat, skins and wool. The skins were employed for parchment, and at an early date wool was sold to London and other markets. In his account for *c.*1420 the bailiff refers to the shearing and packing of lamb's wool and the entry closes with a note that 8s. 4d. was expended on the carriage by water to London of five bales of wool. At Michaelmas 1424 he accounted under 'Sale of Leather Wool and Skins' for 21 sheepskins from sheep which had died of 'murrain' which sold for 12d., and 39s. from the fleeces of 380 lambs. In the Middle Ages sheep were therefore highly profitable, easily manageable, multi-purpose animals.

In comparison with the large flocks of sheep, the number of cattle grazed on the Essex coastal marshlands in the Middle Ages was relatively small. Mention is made in *c.*1420 of two steers being purchased for 38s. and as many calves purchased in May for 45s. Under the heading of 'Dairy' in his 1424 account the bailiff answered for £11 10s. rent from the milk and calves of 46 cows at 5s. a head. He added a note that for the winter months the rent of milk fell to 1s. a cow, which rent was payable to the executors [of the Countess of Hereford]. In addition he answered for 4s. rent from milk only of 1 cow because she had not produced a calf, 10s. rent from milk of 3 heifers, and 12d. rent from milk of 2 heifers being in milk for two weeks only, a total sum for the period Easter–Michaelmas 1424 of £12 5s. Compared with the £32 19s. 6d. rent of milk from the sheep this does not appear to be very much, especially since 46s. relates to rent of calves alone (the cows who had not calved being rented at 4s., the other at 5s. per head, in summer), but the milk production per head was many times greater than the sheep. Indeed, Thorold Rogers, in his *Agriculture and Prices* (1866 edn) states how 'Two cows, according to Walter of Henley's[48] calculations would produce a wey of cheese within this time [Christmas–Michaelmas] besides half a gallon of butter each week', and goes on to state that Walter of Henley 'seems to reckon ten ewes as equal in productiveness to one cow.' This assessment is borne out by the Foulness bailiff's account for 1424 which shows that a milk producing ewe was rented (for milk) at 6d. during the summer months, whereas a cow was rented (for milk) at 4s. in summer and 1s. in winter. Thus cows had the advantage of producing milk for about 8 months of the year – considerably longer than the milking season of ewes. Walter of Henley wrote of cows in his *Husbandry* (*c*.1250)

> If your cows were sorted out, so that the bad were taken away, and your cows fed in pasture of salt marsh, then ought two cows to yield a wey of cheese and half a gallon of butter a week. And twenty ewes which are fed in pasture of salt marsh ought to and can yield cheese and butter as the two cows before named.

During the period Easter–Michaelmas 1424 two cows were sold, one at 8s. because she was unproductive, and six, formerly heifers, were added to the herd, and at Michaelmas there were 60 cows, of which 7 were 'worn-out', within the manor (14 in South Wick, 18 in Nase Wick, 14 in East Wick, 7 in New Wick and 7 in Monkton Barns). In addition there were 2 heifers in South Wick which had grown up from calves, and 2 bullocks in Nase Wick. During the period of the account 1 calf under one year old had been sold and 1 male remained in Nase Wick, and 3 new-born calves were sold and 1 male remained in South Wick. For breeding purposes there were 2 bulls, 1 in South Wick and 1 in Nase Wick.

Other domestic animals within the manor at Michaelmas 1424 included 3 carthorses, 9 'stotts',[49] 1 mated goose and 4 virgin geese, 1 cock and 6 hens, and a number of swans and cygnets.

Contrary to what is normally thought, there was also a considerable amount of arable land within the manor by the fifteenth century. In 1424, 71 acres had been sown with wheat, 21 acres with beans and 71 acres with oats, a total of 163 acres. In addition an unspecified amount of mustard seed was sold for 13s. 4d. Assuming that a 3-course rotation was in operation, the total amount of arable land was probably in the region of 260 acres, or about one-sixth of the demesne, which amounted to about 1,530 acres at this date. It is possible to check this calculation, for under 'Cost of Harvest' in 1424 the bailiff recorded 147 man-days at 6d. per day, paid for on a task basis, for men hired to reap, bind and put into shocks the wheat and oats, a total expenditure of 73s. 6d., and further sums paid on an acreage basis, for reaping, binding and putting in shocks 10½ acres of wheat at 7d. an acre, 8 acres of oats at 6d. an acre, and 21 acres of beans for 16s. *in grosso*. Taking the average cost of reaping, binding and putting in shocks of wheat and oats at 6⅓d. an acre, the total area covered by 'man-day' work was in the region of 135 acres. Added to the 39½ acres worked on an acreage basis a total of about 174½ acres is achieved. But it must be remembered that about one-third of the arable would probably lie fallow every year and so the true figure of arable was likely to be 260 acres. Although the manor of Foulness only comprised about half the island[50] it is unlikely that those mainland manors owning marshes exercised anything more than their rights of pasture. When the crops had been harvested they were stored in 'the grange'. In 1424 the bailiff accounted for an agreement made with one man to stack the crops in the grange for 3s. 4d. This building, of which nothing more is known, the chapel which had been founded in 1386,[51] and 3 fishermen's workshops erected on seawalls,[52] were probably the only permanent buildings within the manor at this date.

The extensive sands off the south and east coasts of Foulness supported an important inshore fishery from which the lord of the manor obtained £9 15s. 4½d. rent for the period Easter to October 1424, for the manor included the offshore sands down to the low-water mark. At Michaelmas 1424 the bailiff accounted for the rents of 57 weirs, 18 kiddells (including 3 'kidelkotes' and 1 'summer kidell'), 10 fisheries *cum hamis et cordis*, 3 workshops built on sea walls and pasture in New Wick for 14 horses. In addition he accounted for several fishing places upon the sands where the method of fishing is not specified, and there is evidence of an oyster fishery in one entry which records that John atte Donne of Burnham paid 10d. for 1 'leyn' next 'le Schore'. Weirs were substantial and permanent structures between high and low water marks, triangular in shape, built of oak posts, six to eight feet high, set several feet apart and thatched with wattling (small pliable lengths of wood and twigs). As the tide fell large numbers of fish, chiefly plaice, dabs, soles and flounders, were trapped in the enclosure and scooped out at low tide and transported back to the shore by horse and cart. Kiddles worked on the same principle but were large square or V-shaped netting enclosures. The *piscaria cum hamis et cordis* were long lines of cord with numerous hooks along their length which were staked out across the sands. As the tide began to flow the hooks were baited and the fish which had been caught were collected at the next ebb.

Most of the fishery was in the hands of a few families from neighbouring mainland parishes, who were undoubtedly professional fishermen. The most prominent family in 1424 was that of 'Thurkyld' which included John, Reginald, Samson and Thomas, who held or had shares in 9 weirs, 12 kiddels, 1 long line and 4 horse pastures. The family of 'atte Bregg' included John, Ralph and Richard and held or had shares in 12 kidells, 11 weirs, 9 long lines and 7 horse pastures. The third of the prominent fishing families was that of Peek which included Ralph senior, Ralph son of John, John son of Ralph, and John son of John, and which held or had shares in 9 weirs, 7 kidells, 1 long line and 4 horse pastures. This family also had a workshop for which Ralph son of John paid 2d. rent for the period Easter–Michaelmas 1424. It measured 40 feet in length, 17 feet in width and stood on an old sea wall (*veterem muru[m]*).

The families involved in the industry must have worked in close co-operation with each other because of the extent to which they shared the fishing appliances. For example, Adrian Bourghild', Reginald Thurkild' Ralph Peek and Richard atte Bregge shared one kiddell called 'Estkidell' in 'le hope' for which they paid 2s. 6d. rent for the period Easter to Michaelmas 1424. They also shared the pasture for 4 horses which cost them 10s. rent for the same period, and a fishery with hooks and cords which cost them 12d. John Kynge of Burnham, John Boter junior, Thomas atte Donne and Richard atte Bregg shared 6 weirs which cost them 10s. for the time of the account.

Apart from defending the island against the sea[53] one of the greatest problems facing the few inhabitants was the lack of a regular supply of fresh water. Rainwater was collected, but 'in hot dry weather became stagnant and extremely unwholesome, causing much sickness and loss'.[54] In order to supplement the rainwater supply, barrels of fresh water had to be brought from the mainland by boat and this activity is mentioned in the medieval bailiffs' accounts. In *c.*1420 the bailiff recorded expenditure of 2s. 4d. on two long ropes of 'bast' [fibrous bark] for mooring the water boats at 'Sundry-schore' and 'Nassewick'. A few years later in 1424 the bailiff recorded under 'Cost of the Boat' the hiring of a carpenter for 4 days to repair 'le waterbot' at 'Sundryschore' for 2s., the purchase of 100 nails called 'bottemenayll' for 20s., 60 nails called 'hoodnayll' for 10d., an unspecified number of nails called 'tynglenayll' for 1d., and 6½ gallons of 'picche' for 3s. 4d., a total of 7s. 10d. In 1486 repairs were made to a watering place called 'le Sesterryn' [cistern] and £4 16s. 1d. was expended on 'the repair of a water boat (*Batild[um] aqu[aticu]m*) in Foulness to carry fresh water for the cattle of the lord's farmers there to take and drink'. The problems arising from the lack of a regular local supply of fresh water were not overcome until the 1830s.[55]

By the end of the Middle Ages the manorial economy of Foulness, as elsewhere, was in decay, and by the mid-16th century the great marshes and wicks, which had formerly been exploited directly for the lord, were let to tenants who farmed on their own account. The period of the Reformation therefore witnessed not only changes in religion and land-ownership, but also a fundamental change in the agricultural economy of the island.

CHAPTER III

LAND OWNERSHIP AND AGRICULTURE:
REFORMATION TO PRESENT DAY

The religious and political complications of the latter half of the reign of Henry VIII, and the reigns of Edward VI and Mary, had a profound effect on land ownership in this country, and in Essex no less than elsewhere. Few men had better opportunities for augmenting their wealth than Sir Richard Rich, created Baron Rich of Leighs in 1548 and Lord Chancellor of England from 1548 to 1551 when he retired from public life due to ill-health. On 25 June 1537 the King granted him New Marsh in the parish of Sutton and Clement Marsh in Little Stambridge[1] which had belonged to the Priory of Leighs before its dissolution earlier that year. Ten years later, on 20 August 1548, Rich sold New Marsh and Clement Marsh to William Harrys[2], who had been the tenant from at least 1532[3], for £560. On 20 November 1549 Rich purchased from Henry Carey, Esq., the

> Manors and farms of Foulnes, Nesshewyke [Nasewick], Arundelles Marsh, Neweyke, Estwyke, Southwyke *alias* Foulnes Hall, Rogworth [Rugwood], Mounkyingebarne *alias* Monkenbarne . . . and the advowson . . . of the church of Foulness.[4]

On Lord Rich's death in 1567 his family was the dominant landed house in Essex, and the vast estates owned by the family, chiefly in Essex, yielded a handsome income. 'A Terrier or Rental of the Possessions of Sir Robert Riche', 2nd Baron Rich of Leighs, drawn up in 1577, gives, *inter alia*, the tenants and rents of the Foulness estate.[5] An abstract is given below.

Farm or Marsh	Tenant	Yearly Rent
		£ s. d.
Shelford	William Bourne	20 12 2
'Monkbarn'	Widow of William Lawson	13 13 4
'Rugworth'	Thomas Rawlyn and Robert Lawson	15 0 0
Moiety of 'Newewick'	Richard Justice	10 16 8
Do.	Robert Justice	10 16 8
'Nassewick'	Thomas and John Harryson	22 0 0
'Estwick'	Edward Bury	14 6 8
Moiety of Southwick *alias* 'Fulnes Hall'	Executors of John Harryson	10 13 4
Do.	Edward Rawlyn	10 13 4
Arundell Marsh	Executors of John Harryson	10 18 8
	TOTAL	139 10 10

15

Although Foulness formed part of the important Rich estates until 1678 very little information about the agriculture and local economy of the island can be discovered before that date. This is readily explained by the fact that when the Rich family estates were divided between six co-heirs in 1678[6] the family archives were apparently likewise divided and only fragments have survived. It has therefore been necessary to draw wholly from printed sources for information.

In 1594 John Norden described Essex as being

> most fatt, frutefull, and full of profitable things exceding (as farr as I can finde) anie other shire, for the general comodeties, and the plentie . . . this shire seemeth to me to deserve this title of the englishe Goshen, the fattest of the Lande; comparable to Palestina, that flowed with milke and hunnye.

Rochford Hundred, in which Foulness lay, he described as yielding

> milke, butter, and cheese in admirable aboundance: and in those partes are the great and huge cheeses made, wondred at for their massivenes and thicknes.

But he also had this to say of the coastal marshlands:

> I can not comende the healthfulnes of it: And especiallie nere the sea coastes, Rochford, Denge, Tendring hundredes and other lowe places about the creekes, which gave me a moste cruell quarterne fever.[7]

It would seem, then, from Norden's description that the coastal marshes were still largely pasture for milk-producing animals and that the dairy industry was still at the base of the marshland economy at the end of the sixteenth century, although there is other evidence to suggest that it was already in decline.

Thirteen years later, in 1607, William Camden had much the same thing to say of the marshlands, which were

> plentifull in grasse, and rich in Cattaile, but Sheepe especially where all their doing is in making of Cheese: and there shall ye have men take the womens office in hand and milke Ewes: whence those huge thicke Cheeses are made that are vented and sould not onely into all parts of England, but into forraign nations also, for the rusticall people, labourers, and handicraftes men to fill their bellies, and feed upon.

And describing Canvey Island, he wrote 'we have seen youths . . . milk, with small stools fastened to their buttocks, and make ewes' cheeses in those cheese sheds which they call there 'wiches'.[8]

On the death in 1673 of Charles Rich, 4th Earl of Warwick, the vast family estates passed to his widow Mary, there being no male heir. On her death in 1678 the estate was split between six co-heirs and the Rochford estate, which included Foulness, came into the hands of Daniel Finch, 2nd Earl of Nottingham[9], who had married Lady Essex Rich, second daughter of the 4th Earl of Warwick and Mary Rich. The ownership of the manor of Foulness was to remain in the hands of the Finch family until 1915.[10]

In 1688 a detailed survey and rental of the Foulness estate[11] was prepared for Daniel Finch (see Appendix for an abstract). The rents totalled £1,351 per annum and a total of 259 acres on five farms had been 'inned' from the sea during 1687–88.[12] But more important is the decline of the dairies or 'wicks', and the considerable increase in the proportion of arable land. On Priestwood marsh 90 acres out of a total of 275 were arable, and on New Wick marsh, which contained 221 acres, 75 acres, or rather more than one-third, were under the plough. The highest proportion of all was on Arundel Marsh and Ridge Marsh, where a total of 360 acres was farmed by Peter Porter, of which 138 acres, or two-fifths, were arable. The lowest proportions of arable were at Shelford Marsh, in the extreme west of the island, where of a total of 545 acres it was only permissible to plough 100 acres, and at Nase Wick Marsh where of a total of 420 acres only five or six were in tillage.

The marshes with the higher proportions of arable land were those 'inned' from the saltings (Arundel Marsh, Ridge Marsh and New Wick) while those with the lower proportions were at the west, south-west and north-west corner of the island where the soil is composed of a heavier clay. Nase Wick must be regarded as a separate case for there is evidence to suggest that it was intentionally kept as pasture and it is known that the Finch family grazed their own animals on it during 1685–86.[13] Thus as early as the seventeenth century the superior qualities of the 'inned' land, with its highly fertile and easily worked aluvium soil, were fully recognised.

It is not easy to supply reasons for the decline of the dairy farming, but it would seem to have begun as early as the middle of the sixteenth century, and a clue is given by William Harrison, the parson of the Essex parish of Radwinter, when he writes in his chapter on 'the Food and Diet of the English'

> . . . white meats, as milk, butter, and cheese, which were never so dear as in my time and wont to be accounted of as one of the chief stays throughout the island, are now reputed as food appertinent only to the inferior sort, whilst such as are more wealthy do feed upon the flesh of all kinds of cattle accustomed to be eaten, all sorts of fish taken upon our coasts and in our fresh rivers, and such diversity of wild and tame fowls as are either bred in our island or brought over unto us from other countries in the main.[14]

One recent major work on the agricultural history of this country has gone so far as to say that during the period 1500–1640 'In addition to their grazing pastures, all the Essex marshland parishes had extensive cornlands.' It goes on to cite the Thames-side marshland parish of Aveley, which in 1619 contained 2,249½ acres of demesnes and farms of which 889¾ acres were pasture and 700½ acres were arable. In other words, 31 per cent of the land was in corn.[15] Further evidence of the decline of dairies is contained in the survey of the greater part of Foulness compiled for Daniel Finch in 1688. It contains under each of the farms details of tithes payable, both to the incumbent of Foulness and to those of the mainland parishes in which the respective marshes formerly lay. On eight farms the tithes included two cheeses but for seven the entry reads 'two cheese if any made', indicating that production of this commodity had largely ceased by the second half of the seventeenth century.

The proportion of arable land continued to increase steadily after 1688. In 1699 Nasewick was leased to Richard Nott and John Collins for 21 years at £170 per annum, with liberty to break up 60 acres for tillage. Five years later the farm was let to John Raim and James Nott for 21 years at £170 per annum and on 12 July 1704 they signed a separate agreement to allow them to break up a further 40 acres in return for an increase in rent of £30 per annum. The 'west-end' of Shelford Marsh was let to John Wright from Michaelmas 1700 for 21 years at £93 10s. per annum, with liberty to plough 30 acres, while John Lodwick was allowed to increase the amount of arable at the 'east-end' of Shelford from 100 to 120 acres in 1698 for no increase in rent.[16]

The survey of 1688 also provides details of the husbandry clauses contained in the leases, and they follow a standard pattern with only minor variations. The tenants were to keep and leave all buildings in good repair and were to maintain the sea walls, ditches and sluices. All dung was to be spread, none to be burnt or removed. Arable land was not to be miseasoned, that is, to neglect or misuse the arable so as to make it impoverished or destitute, no more than two consecutive crops could be taken, and it was to lay fallow one year in three. No mustard seed, cole seed 'or other unusual seed' was to be sown without special permission and for every acre of land ploughed in excess of the stipulated amount of arable a penalty of £5 a year was payable.[17]

While dairy farming was declining in the coastal marshlands it was developing on a smaller scale in south-west Essex around Epping, Kelvedon Hatch, Navestock, Lambourne, Stanford Rivers, Ongar and the Theydons,[18] encouraged by proximity to London. The rich marshland grazing became used

17

for fattening sheep and cattle, particularly during the summer months, from where they were taken to London for slaughter.[19] But this was ancillary to wheat growing; the output of which, already large in 1700, was to rise steadily throughout the eighteenth century.[20] By 1700 it is probable that about one-third of Foulness had been converted to arable, the greatest product of which was wheat, grown for the London market. It was shipped by sailing barges from the quay at Monkton Barns and other 'hards' on which the flat-bottomed sailing barges could settle between tides. Indeed the 'conveniency of water carriage' was one of the island's greatest economic assets, particularly in view of the high cost of road transport. As Mr. A. F. J. Brown has shown, 'When farms near the coast were advertised, proximity to sea transport was a major recommendation.'[21]

In 1740–42 Foulness was described as being

> fruitful, producing good Corn of all kinds but the water brackish, being impregnated by the Salt of the Earth: They have none perfectly fresh but rainwater, preserved in Cisterns. The fences are only ditches, which every tide fills. Over these, as in other Marshes what they call *Wolves* are laid, upon which their Gates are fixed. Eight Hours in twelve their is Passage for a Horse to *Wakering*.[22] The Houses are all of Wood, which soon decay, through the Inclemency (as the Inhabitants say) of the Air. To the same Cause they ascribe the ill thriving of their fruit Trees: The latter seems owing to the abundant Salt with which the Staple is loaded: and perhaps the first may be attributed to the same sapping Quality. If the air were chargeable with all this, the People could not bear it so well as they do.[23]

By the mid-eighteenth century the amount of arable had probably exceeded that of pasture for the first time. The estate records of the Finch family (or other Foulness landowners) have not survived for this period, but a lease of Great Burwood Farm is preserved. On 1 March 1762 it was leased to Edward Kennitt of Foulness, yeoman, for a term of 21 years at a rent of £95 a year. The farm comprised about two hundred acres of which only sixty were pasture. The arable land was to lie fallow every third year and for every acre of pasture put under the plough an additional annual rent of £5 was payable. The tenant was responsible for the maintenance and repair of the farm buildings, scouring and cleansing the ditches, and the upkeep of the sea walls. All muck, dung or compost was to be spread on the land 'in a husband like manner', and any straw or hay not used for fodder was to belong to the landlord, but if this clause was not complied with 40s. was payable for every cart-load of hay taken away or otherwise removed from the premises, for straw 20s. and for muck, dung or compost 5s.[24] There is nothing exceptional or unusual in these husbandry clauses; they are absolutely typical for the region and period. The rent of 9s. 6d. an acre was about average for south-east Essex in the mid-eighteenth century.[25]

If the proportions of arable and pasture on Great Burwood farm in 1762 can be taken as representative of the whole island, it would appear that only 30 per cent of Foulness remained under grass by the third quarter of the 18th century. Indeed, this may be an underestimate, for Great Burwood lies at the south-western end of the island, where the soil is less productive than elsewhere and where a comparatively larger proportion of pasture would therefore be expected. In 1794 it seemed as if the standard of farming in south-east Essex was

> as near, if not nearer, perfection than in any other part of Essex. The land is in general of a deep, rich, tender, loamy quality, and as in other parts, rather farmed than grazed. The crops of wheat, beans, oats, coleseed or rape, mustard, and in short of any thing that is sown, afford a great return . . .[26]

Arthur Young, the greatest of all English writers on agriculture and Secretary of the Board of Agriculture in 1793, published his *General View of the Agriculture of the County of Essex* in 1813, and it is undoubtedly the most valuable source of information on the agriculture of Essex in the late eighteenth and early nineteenth centuries. 'Foulness Island', he wrote, 'I am much inclined to think the richest soil in this county. The following is a note I made on it many years ago.'

> Forty years ago the whole was under water,[27] and no corn got for two years; but after that much greater than ever, so as to furnish an effectual proof that the water did good, after being chastened and corrected by the atmosphere . . . The fertility of it is so great, that the farmers are very little attentive to dung.[28]

On the lack of a regular supply of fresh water he had this to say

> . . . the only supply for drinking is to be obtained from the rain, or from the melted snows: this forms but a precarious and scanty dependence, which in the summer season is frequently dried up, or by putrefaction rendered extremely injurious to the health of the inhabitants and too frequently also to that of the horses and cattle: hence there are but few resident occupiers in the islands; and in particular dry seasons, the larger stock are driven from Foulness to Shoebury for water . . .[29]

Fresh water was also brought on to the island from Great Wakering, a distance of six or seven miles.[30]

Young found the average rent on Foulness to be 25s. an acre, the tenants of the Finch family paying 23s. 6d.[31] The average for south-east Essex during 1791–1815 was 20s. 3d.[32] The leases on the farms owned by Finch were of 21 years, but Young tells us this was general in the Rochford Hundred.[33]

For the purpose of productivity, Foulness is not treated individually by Young, but as one of the 'Marsh Islands' of the archipelago. The following table, based on his *Agriculture of Essex*,[34] illustrates clearly the high fertility and productivity of the islands.

Crop	Bushels per acre— County Average	Bushels per acre— 'Marsh Islands'
Wheat	24½	30
Oats	36½	40
Beans	27	32

Mustard, which in 1688 was regarded as 'unusual'[35] and could not be grown without the landlord's permission, became a common crop on Foulness during the eighteenth century. Charles Vancouver, the famous American agriculturist, had this to say of it in 1795:

> In the islands of Foulness, Wallasea, etc., and in the embanked marshes, white or brown mustard seed is sown; one peck and a half per acre on an oat-stubble. Cutting and thraving the seed are done at 10s. 6d. per acre; thrashing is done on a sheet in the field, at 5s. per quarter: mean produce twenty-four bushels per acre.
>
> 1784. Foulness. Very profitable here, 3, 4, and even 5 qrs. [per acre] at £4 [per quarter].[36]

At Widford, the other centre of mustard growing in Essex, a farmer considered himself very lucky to achieve 4 quarters per acre in 1801, on well-prepared ground.[37]

Of manuring on Foulness, Young wrote:

> . . . of all the countries I have seen, this is the worst provided for making dung; in many miles I did not see one farmyard in the Island, or any thing like an enclosure for confining cattle: the appearance was that of barns opening to the waste, with straw at the doors, and the cattle free to wander where they pleased. The great fertility of the soil takes off all anxiety upon this subject; and within the memory of man, dung was not thought worth carting on to the land.[38]

Welsh and Scottish cattle were the chief breeds kept on Foulness, but the 'number of cows kept on the island is very inconsiderable'.[39] Sheep were more numerous and 'the whole stock were Lincolns: ten or twelve years ago there was not a South-down in the Isle; now many, and increasing'.[40]

It has been shown that in 1762 on Great Burwood farm the arable land was worked for two years and lay fallow on the third.[41] This was the same as on Daniel Finch's farms in 1688[42], but in 1784 on his property Arthur Young found the course to be 1 fallow, 2 beans, 3 wheat, 4 beans, 5 wheat, and sometimes oats added. By the early nineteenth century the leases stipulated the following rotation, proposed by the estate manager, a Mr. Wood: 1 fallow, 2 oats, barley, or white mustard, 3 clover, 4 wheat, 5 beans or peas, 6 wheat. Should the clover fail, beans were to be grown in lieu of it.[43]

During the second half of the eighteenth century and up to 1815 the tenant farmers with larger holdings (above about 200 acres) flourished, and many with marshland farms resided in the more healthy and congenial upland areas. Young noted that:

> Only two farmers live in the island . . . the rest . . . employ *lookers*, who are paid 12s. to 14s. a week; have a cow kept; pigs; their rent free, and one or two cauldrons of coals.[44]

For centuries the Essex coastal marshlands were regarded as unhealthy or even dangerous for humans. As has already been shown,[45] John Norden complained in the sixteenth century of 'the sea coastes, Rochford, Denge, Tendring hundredes and other lowe places about the creeks, which gave me a most cruell quarterne fever'[46] and one hundred and fifty years later Daniel Defoe described how when people came 'into the marshes among the fogs and damps, there they presently changed their complexion [and] got an ague or two . . .'[47] Young himself noted the 'ravages of agues and autumnal fevers' which were prevalent on Foulness.

> I asked, I believe, thirty persons if they had had agues, and every one answered in the affirmative, in a tone and manner that marked sufficiently how common and universal they were.[48]

For centuries the lack of a regular supply of fresh water had caused inconvenience both to man and beast.[49] Attempts had been made to alleviate the problem in 1725 when a well was sunk on Great Shelford Marsh to a depth of 92 feet, but without success.[50] In the late eighteenth century unsuccessful attempts were made by Francis Bannester, the owner of neighbouring Rushley Island, to obtain fresh water by boring, and his descendant, also Francis Bannester,

> long felt the want of a regular supply of good water, having none for the use of the inhabitants or stock but what was obtained in rainy seasons, and which in hot dry weather becomes stagnant and extremely unwholesome, causing much sickness and loss.[51]

In 1828, realising the possibility of obtaining fresh water by boring, Bannester began his work on Rushley Island, and on 1 January 1829 he struck fresh water at a depth of almost 500 feet. By 1834 more than twenty springs were serving the six islands of the Essex archipelago[52] and by 1889 wells had been sunk on fourteen Foulness farms.[53]

In 1847 the tithes payable by Foulness farmers were commuted for money payment under the provisions of the General Tithe Act 1836, and the award, schedule and map prepared for the tithe commutation commission[54] form a complete land utilisation survey of the island at that time. It comprised a total area of 6,310 acres of which 425 were saltings. The area within (and including) sea walls was 5,885 acres, and because no reclamation has taken place since 1833[55] the area within the perimeter walls is the same today. There were 4,544 acres of arable land, 783 acres of pasture[56] and 338 acres of inland water (drainage ditches, ponds, etc.). The remaining 222 acres comprised houses, barns, farmyards, church and churchyard, sea walls and chases, cottages and gardens, and waste land. Those farms with highest proportions of pasture were Small Ports, Priestwood and Rugwood, while New House and Tree (formerly part of New House) farms, which were largely on 'inned' land showed the greatest proportions of arable. The chief crops were wheat, barley, oats, beans, white mustard and clover.[57]

In 1875 began the long national depression in agriculture, caused by massive importation of cheap American wheat. Essex, with its reliance on wheat, was particularly hard hit, and established farming families failed in hundreds. Farms were left on landlords' hands, vast acreages of productive land reverted to rough pasture, and rents declined sharply. The *Royal Commission on Agriculture* (Essex) 1894, does not specifically mention Foulness, but a map of 1880 appended to the report shows that about one-quarter of the land in Dengie and Rochford Hundreds had reverted to pasture, but that no land on Foulness had been so affected. This superficial evidence would suggest that Foulness escaped the worst effects of the depression. An examination of the 19th-century deeds of Great Burwood Farm has revealed that no land on that farm reverted to rough pasture. In 1858, at the peak of agricultural prosperity, the farm comprised 386 acres of which only about 47 were pasture. By 1899 the farm comprised 389 acres, and, rather surprisingly, the proportion of arable had increased, for only about 12 acres were pasture. But the value of the land had slumped dramatically; in 1858 it sold for £11,165, but in 1899 it only made £1,800.[58]

The opening of the twentieth century was to herald a new era in the story of Foulness, and for the first time in their history agriculture and fishing were soon to share the island with a less peaceful industry. As early as 1855 the War Department had established an artillery practice and testing range at South Shoebury, overlooking the extensive Shoebury Sands, a continuation of the Maplins.[59] The value of Foulness and the Maplin Sands as a weapons research and development centre was seen by the Government, and by the end of the nineteenth century the decision had been taken to acquire the island and its offshore sands. In 1900 a portion of the Foulness Sands north-ward of Fishermans Head was acquired, but the rest of the sands, down to low water mark, remainded the property of the lord of the manor, Mr. Alan G. Finch. Negotiations with Finch to secure shooting rights over the sands in 1912 were frustrated when it was discovered that large portions were leased to copyhold tenants for fishing kiddles. The War Department then sought to acquire the lordship of the manor of Foulness which would enable them to extinguish all copyhold interests on the sands either by purchase or as they fell vacant, but Finch refused to sell. However, after his death in 1914 the manor passed to a half-brother, Wilfred Henry Montgomery Finch, who immediately entered into negotiations and sold the lordship on 13 July 1915.[60] With the ownership of the lordship, the ancient demesne lands of the manor, which comprised about two-thirds of the island, came into the hands of the War Department. At the same time the Department had been busy purchasing those farms not within the manor of Foulness, and by about the end of the First World War the whole island with the exception of the church, rectory, the mission hall at Courts End and the school, had one owner. Today, five large farming concerns share the island with the Armed Forces.

The present day agriculture of Foulness is perhaps the most productive in Essex, due to the natural richness of the soil and the high standard of farming on the island. The current national average yield for wheat is 30.5 cwt. per acre, but output on the island is consistently in excess of this, and the figures for the 1967–68 harvest of one of the five farming concerns was close on two tons an acre, or almost a third above average. Barley is also an important crop on Foulness, and the yield per acre is comfortably in excess of the national average of 28.2 cwt. per acre. Apart from wheat and barley the island also produces excellent crops of beans, peas and mustard, the latter having been grown there since before 1424. From the rich pastures come quantities of beef and mutton, and, of course, wool.

Not only is Foulness agriculturally outstanding for quantity, but also for quality. The mustard crop has regularly drawn letters of commendation from a well-known mustard firm and in 1958 a prize for wheat was won in the Royal Winter Fair at Toronto. In the Southern Area competition run by the *Farmer's Weekly*, prizes for biscuit wheat and bread wheat were won in 1958 and 1962 respectively. Some of the many prizes won at county level in recent years were a gold medal for milling wheat in 1958–59, prizes for feeding and tie beans, millable oats, feeding barley and milling wheat in 1966, and in 1967 prizes for malting barley, feeding beans, millable oats and milling wheat.

Although kiddle fishing on the off-shore sands was extinguished after the Ministry of Defence had acquired Foulness in 1915 many islanders still set 'bands' (long lines), and when the Ministry leaves Foulness and firing across the sands ceases there is no reason why the kiddle fishing industry should not be resurrected. Although to the unfamiliar eye the sands may appear a desolate waste they do in fact support a vast quantity of marine life, and in particular the common cockle. This small nutritious shellfish inhabits most of the surface, reaching in places over a million to the acre, and approximately two-thirds of the nation's supply of cockles come from these sands. In 1964 the harvest amounted to 43,574 cwt. On the edge of the Maplin Sands lies the only commercial whiteweed bed in Europe. This small industry earns considerable foreign exchange, much of its produce being exported to the United States.[61]

CHAPTER IV

THE PARISH AND CHURCH

Foulness, although now a separate ecclesiastical parish, was originially parcelled among and paid tithes to the neighbouring parishes of Rochford, Sutton, Little Wakering, Shopland and Little Stambridge,[1] all in Rochford Hundred.[2]

The inhabitants of Foulness and other marshland areas were expected to attend divine service at their respective parish churches, often many miles away, but in practice it must often have been impossible, and certainly extremely inconvenient, for them to attend. By 1386 a chapel had been established on the island for the convenience of its few shepherd inhabitants by Lady Joan de Bohun, Countess of Essex, Hereford and Northampton, and lady of the manor, by the authority of Richard Gifford, Bishop of London.[3] But it 'had then but little Endowment, and the Chaplain made little or no residence there'[4] and in 1407 Lady Joan obtained a licence for the payment of 100s.

> to found a chantry of one chaplain to celebrate divine service daily in a chapel built in the island called Foulness . . . and to grant in mortmain to the chaplain a rood of land on which the chapel is situated, an acre of land for his mansion to be built upon and a messuage and certain land and marsh called Litelbourewerde [Little Burwood] containing 80 acres of fresh land and 160 acres of salt marsh and 33s. 4d. rent from the manor of Foulnesse, held in chief.[5]

The chaplain was to receive all the tithes, oblations and spiritual profits that formerly belonged to the ministers of the mainland parishes, payable from the inhabitants of the island, and the right of patronage was vested in the lord of the manor.[6]

In 1545 or 1547 the Chantry was dissolved under Stat. 37 Hen. VIII c.4 or Stat. I Edw. VI c.14, and all its land and revenues were declared to belong to the Crown. Foulness became a separate ecclesiastical parish and rectory, the old chantry chapel was demolished and a new timber-framed parish church dedicated to St Mary the Virgin was erected on the site. It had a spire with a vestry below, in which was a fireplace, the smoke escaping through a hole in the top of the spire. It was a small building, measuring only 40 feet in length and 20 feet in width.[7]

Despite the island becoming a separate ecclesiastical parish, its inhabitants had to pay great tithes to the parishes in which they formerly lay until all the island's tithes were commuted for money payment in 1847. Whilst no doubt extremely inconvenient and annoying to Foulness people at the time, the survival of these ancient payments until the middle of the nineteenth century and the existence of the commutation schedule, has made it possible to reconstruct the ancient parochial divisions of the island with a high degree of accuracy.[8] Only in the case of the original area of East Wick does the award fail to name one of the five mainland parishes among which the island was originally divided. Yet this is not surprising, for the tithe apportionment map shows East Wick to be almost wholly on 'inned' land, a position incompatible with its medieval existence. The original location of East Wick had been known from the end of the sixteenth century as Great Lodge, from about 1650 as Old Lodge Marsh and in the nineteenth century as Lodge Farm. The confusion arose during the years 1577–83; in 1577 the tenant at East Wick was Edward Bury,[9] but six years later he was stated to be tenant at 'Great Lodge'[10], no doubt a recently constructed dwelling-house. By chance the name East Wick survived in an area to the south of Great Lodge. Perhaps because of confusion arising from the change in name, or perhaps by earlier commutation of tithes payable to a mainland parish, the tenant at Lodge Farm in 1847 was only paying tithes to the rector of Foulness, and therefore the ancient mainland parish in which the farm lay was not stated. It was possible, however, to identify it from the mainland parish given in the tithe commutation award for Foxes Farm, which had been carved out of the original area of East Wick in the eighteenth century and which continued to pay tithes – to Sutton.[11]

By the early nineteenth century the old church was in a bad state of repair and inadequate for the needs of a parish whose population was expanding rapidly. At a meeting of the parishioners in April 1848 it was resolved 'That the old church be pulled down, and a new church erected'.[12] The old church was demolished in 1850 and the present church of St Mary the Virgin erected to the designs of William Hambley a short distance to the west of the original site at a cost of £2,000, of which £800 was provided by the parishioners, £400 by George Finch Esq., the lord of the manor and patron of the living, £295 by two ecclesiastical building societies, and the remaining £505 by private subscription, including £50 from the Elder Brethren of Trinity House for the spire to be built sufficiently high to serve as a landfall for mariners. The consecration by the Bishop of Rochester of the new church and additional ground taken into the churchyard, which had been given by George Finch, took place on 3 July 1853.[13] The stone building is in the Early English Style, with spire, nave with two aisles, and chancel. When built it contained 350 sittings.[14] It is severely plain within and has no stained glass.

In the late eighteenth and early nineteenth centuries Foulness was fortunate in having four outstanding ministers. In 1771 Thomas Ellwood was appointed curate, a post which he held for 41 years before being made rector in 1813. He wore 'low shoes with buckles, velvet breeches, with silver buckles to knees, wig, in which he slept, straight collared frock coat with a turned-up hat and a rosette in front.' He died on 18 April 1815, aged 74, and was buried in the chancel of the old church.[15] His affection for the parish in which he had lived so long was shown by the provision in his will of £100, upon trust

> that the half-yearly interest thereof should be . . . distributed on Good Friday and the feast of St. Thomas the Apostle by the minister and churchwarden among idigent persons belonging to this parish who received no parochial relief.[16]

Ellwood was succeeded by Thomas Archer, who in 1815 was already 65 years of age. He was a scholarly and eloquent preacher, as well as a great cross-country rider and heavy smoker. He died in February 1832, aged 82 years, and, like Ellwood, was buried in the chancel of the old church. His monument declares him to have been 'a friend of the poor'.[17]

In 1844 Harvey Vachell became rector and 'set about reforming the manners and morals of the inhabitants'. During his short incumbency (he resigned the living at Michaelmas 1847) many lasting improvements in the standard of behaviour and morals of the inhabitants took place.[18] The living was next accepted by the Rev. Samuel Neale Dalton, M.A., 'a man of primitive and retiring manners' and who 'like his predecessor, has employed his time in carrying on the good work commenced as auspiciously.'[19]

Today the church is poorly attended and suffering badly from rising damp. The Rector, the Rev. Sidney Powley, lives at Thorpe Bay, and the old rectory is let to tenants.

CHAPTER V

DEFENCE AGAINST THE SEA, FLOODING AND 'INNING'

It has already been shown[1] that since the end of the last Ice Age, south-east England has been steadily sinking relative to sea level. Although most of Foulness now lies well below the level of high water, it is unlikely that there was any need to embank it during the period of Romano–British settlement.[2] Indeed, the Domesday assessment of the marshes as 'pasture for sheep' does not imply that they were embanked or reclaimed, and the Langenhoe marshes, which in 1086 were reckoned capable of supporting 600 sheep, were still unembanked as late as 1414.[3] Because the marshes were unprotected the bailiffs' accounts for the manor of Langenhoe, which survive for the period 1324–1440,[4] clearly show that protection had to be given to the sheep. They frequently record payments for 'schepes bregges' (sheep's bridges) made of 'flakis' (wattle hurdles) and for 'pettynges' (raised causeways of peat sods, often hundreds of yards long) to allow the sheep to escape when an exceptionally high tide rose deep on the saltings and marshes.

Nevertheless, elsewhere on the low-lying Essex coast it had been necessary to embank parts of the marshlands as early as the end of the 12th century, and probably earlier. The *Anglo Saxon Chronicle* records that in 1099 on the Festival of St. Martin (11 November) 'the sea-flood sprung up to such a height and did so much harm as no man remembered that it ever did before'. Even the Romans experienced the occasional monstrous tide, for in A.D. 31 they were forced to abandon their coastal station and withdraw to higher ground at the settlement at Shoeburyness.[5] By 1210 the 'law of the marsh' embodied the important principle that each man should contribute to the upkeep of defences from which he benefited, in proportion to his land or rights on the marsh, a principle which was to endure until the passing of the Land Drainage Act, 1930. In the thirteenth century, documentary references to sea defences become much more frequent and reflect the growing concern of both officialdom and local landowner to the threat 'of that unmerciful enemy the Sea', and before the end of the century supervision of the coastal defences was in the hands of certain king's justices and other dignitaries, specially appointed from time to time under temporary commissions 'of walls and ditches (*de Walliis et Fossatis*)'. In 1280 under the first known commission specifically appointed for Essex, the sheriff of Essex was commanded by Edward I to distrain on any neighbours of the Abbot of Stratford who did not maintain their banks and ditches in the marshes of West Ham. In the following century over 50 Essex commissions were enrolled, many being concerned with the banks of the upper reaches of Thames-side. Others were directed into different parts of the county and several included Foulness; in 1303 a commission was directed to the 'sea coast of Essex', in 1328 'alongside the Thames and part adjacent', in 1331 to the hundreds of Dengie and Rochford; and in the years 1335, 1338 and 1346 to Rochford hundred, in which Foulness lay.

These commissions were not mere formalities, but had real powers; they were normally required to survey the sea defences in a thorough fashion; to discover those persons responsible for disrepair or decay, and those who benefitted by the defences and to rate all such persons to pay for the maintenance or repair in proportion to their acres or rights in the area; to audit the accounts for repairs; to hear and determine any disputes; and to compel any negligent or 'rebellious' persons to carry out their obligations.

While it is not possible to determine when it first became necessary to embank Foulness against the sea, it was certainly some time before 1271, for the Charter Rolls of that year contain the earliest known documentary reference to sea walls on the island.[6] By 1348 much, if not all, of the island lay below the level of ordinary high tides for in that year 'a marsh called Litleburghwerth' (Little Burwood – one of the 11 or 12 large marshes into which Foulness was then subdivided) was described as being 'daily inundated by the sea'.[7] Although the cause is not stated it was almost certainly the result of a breach in the sea defences. The important point is that the marsh was 'daily inundated'; in other words it was covered by every tide and not just by exceptionally high spring tides.

The earliest surviving bailiff's account of the manor of Foulness, c.1420, mentions the sea defences. Expenses of 2s. 6d. were incurred in making 12 'hurdles' of twigs cut in the wood called 'Leye' for the repair of 'Sundryschore' and 20d. for the hire of 5 men for 1 day to dig the ground and lay the hurdles and thereby heighten 'le Schore'.[8] The walls themselves were of earth, and therefore very susceptible to weathering by sea, wind and rain. In order to afford them some protection they were thatched with brushwood or rushes made into faggots or hurdles[9]. This was the usual method of medieval sea wall construction.

In 1424 the bailiff recorded the payment of 2d. by Ralph, son of John Peek, for a site, 40 feet along and 17 feet wide, on the old [sea] wall (*veterem muru[m]*) on the west of 'la Ferthyngkote', for a workshop to be built thereon.[10] The description of the wall as 'old' lends further weight to the evidence that Foulness was already embanked before 1271. The practice of building houses on old sea walls, which afford a firm base, away from the damp, and high enough to offer some protection in case of flooding, has endured to modern times. Mention of the walls in the bailiff's accounts is made again in 1486, and in 1498–99 when a total of £4 16s. 2d. was spent in repairs.[11]

It would be a mistake to think of Foulness as being defended against the sea during the Middle Ages only by one great wall running round the perimeter of the island. The island was made up of thirteen large marshes or wicks, all of which have been identified[12]; they were Shelford Marsh, Great and Little Burwood, Clement Marsh, New Marsh, Rugwood Marsh, Priestwood Marsh, Monkton Barns Marsh, South Wick (Foulness Hall Marsh), Nase Wick, East Wick, New Wick ('inned' by c.1420) and Arundel Marsh ('inned' between 1424 and 1486). It is doubtful whether there were any other marshes before sub-division of those listed above began in the sixteenth century. Although marshes are sometimes called by other names which cannot be identified, for example, 'Pertrichesmershe', 'Thurkellesmershe' (the family of Thurkyld is mentioned in the bailiff's account of 1424) and 'Gorgotes mershe', the explanation is almost certainly that the scribe referred to the marsh not by its proper name, but by that of its tenant or owner. Moreover the thirteen marsh names appear fairly continuously over a period of several centuries, whereas unidentifiable names occur once or twice in a short period, but do not reappear. Each of these marshes was independently protected against the sea, being completely enclosed by a wall, so that if the sea defences of one marsh failed, the others would not be flooded. Many of these ancient internal or 'counter' walls are still to be seen on the island.

Between the internal walls ran deep ditches connected to the sea by sluices in the perimeter walls. On every tide the sea rose and fell in these ditches, so that at high water Foulness was sub-divided into a number of smaller islands. Most of the sluices have now been blocked but the sea is periodically allowed to enter through the remaining sluices to cleanse the ditches. The salt content of the water in the ditches varies considerably; after a period of heavy rain it is slight, but increases when sea water is used for flushing.

A comparison with Canvey Island is valuable, for it reveals clearly the events which led to the walling of Foulness before 1271. Like Foulness, Canvey was prized for its valuable pasture and was an important centre of dairy farming, producing great quantities of cheese, butter and milk. References to the construction of a sea wall occur in the bailiff's accounts of the manor of Southchurch; 38s. 6d. was spent on making 154 perches of sea wall in 1437 and 13s. 4d. was spent making 80 perches in 1438.[13] Southchurch was one of the nine mainland parishes among which Canvey was divided, and the walls mentioned in the accounts would relate only to those parts belonging to Southchurch. Whether there had been any attempt to wall the whole island before the 17th century is still an open question, but it is quite clear from the writings of late 16th-century topographers and from contemporary maps, that Canvey was disintegrating into several small islands, separated from each other by channels and 'guts'. In 1577 William Harrison explored the Essex coast by boat and described Canvey as the 'Canwaie Iles, which some call marshes onelie', dissected by the 'salt rilles also that crosse the same . . .'[14] In the last edition of his *Britannia*, published in 1607, William Camden wrote of Canvey

> It is indeed so low-lying, that often it is all overflown, except for the higher hillocks, on which there is a safe retreat for the sheep . . .[15]

There can be little doubt that the same sort of events had occurred on Foulness, but somewhat earlier. The boundaries of the great medieval marshes were in many cases delineated by small creeks or 'guts' which every tide filled, and were a further reason why it was necessary to wall each marsh independently.

In 1532, 'A Generall Acte concernynge Commissions of Sewers to be directed in all partes within the Realme'[16] laid down in a standard form the powers and duties of the commissioners and courts of sewers, and the machinery for maintaining defences under commission. Although the jurisdiction of the commissioners and courts remained limited to sea defence and land drainage in the area covered by their commissioner, increased emphasis was placed on the powers of the commissioners to carry out the work themselves, as distinct from compelling those responsible to do it. It has already been shown that Foulness had been included in commissions from the beginning of the fourteenth century, but few other details are known. After the act of 1532 the island continued to be included in temporary commissions, but not always, it seems, to the agreement of the inhabitants. In *c*.1695 Foulness was included in 'A Commission of Sewers for the Hundreds of Rochford, Chelmsford and Dengy and the Islands of Foulnesse Potton etc.' The inhabitants were so annoyed that they should be included 'without the privity and contrary to the desire of the Earle of Notingham the Principall Proprietor or any other Proprietor . . . or any of their Tenants' that they engaged the services of the famous lawyer, St. John Brodrick.[17] They argued that since

> The Nature of these Islands is such that they cannot hurt or prejudice any part of the said Levell by their Breaches nor be hurt themselves by any inundatons of water that may happen to any other part of the Levell . . .

that they would not be 'benefited by any Comission of Sewers or hurt for want of one.' They complained that in 1690

> An extraordinary Spring Tyde happended and layd these Islands under water as well as Some other parts of the Country and then the Propietors Repaired at their own Charge without any help or assistance of a Comission of Sewers and that So substantially that in all likelyhood they may never be overflowed as before.

The Commissioners, it was claimed, 'have taxed and received great Sum[m]es of Mony towards the expences and Charges of the Comission have done no publique repairs but wasted it all in eating and drinking . . .' Brodrick replied, stating the legal position in some detail, but the most important and interesting remark was that he could not

> think of any method so likely to deliver the islands from such oppressions for the future. As to sue to my Ld Keeper[18] for a particular Commission for these Islands, which being once granted, and consequently an Order obtained for the leaving them out of the General Commission, there will be no need of renewing that Commission, or danger of inserting them again in the general Commission, until there is some Petition or Complaint for want of Care.[19]

But it was not until 1800 that Foulness was placed under a separate Commission, which was to endure for more than a century, and it is obvious from the numerous presentments of the early sessions of the commissioners that the sea defences were in poor condition. For example, at the fourth meeting, held on 8 June 1801 it was presented that the sea defences of ten farms were 'out of repair and not sufficient to defend the Land and Tenements . . . from the violence of the Sea . . .' A marsh lot of one shilling per acre was imposed at the meeting on 29 January 1801; this produced about £250 per annum and was used to pay the expenses of the Commission, entertainment and refreshment for the Commissioners, the expenses and salaries of the clerk and marsh bailiff, and for a survey and map of the island, which cost £136 9s. 0d.[20] In 1804 the rate was reduced to 6d. per acre. The Reverend Henry Bate Dudley of Bradwell-juxta-Mare was appointed a commissioner in 1800, and was elected chairman of several of the early meetings, no doubt because of his experience in reclaiming 250 acres of marsh at East Hall Farm in Bradwell-juxta-Mare, (and elsewhere in that parish and neighbouring Tillingham) which was much admired by his contemporaries. The commission levied no general rate in order to pay for repairs, but employed a marsh bailiff who presented to the jurors at the meetings details of any sea defences which were 'out of repair'. The owner of the farm was then informed of what needed to be done and was given a reasonable amount of time in which to have the necessary repairs carried out, on penalty of a fine, which appears to have been the marsh bailiff's estimate of the cost of the work, to be paid into the Exchequer.

It has already been shown that Foulness, as it existed in the Middle Ages, comprised a number of marshes, each with its own defensive walls, erected at an early date.[21] To this 'original' part of the island successive 'innings' over several centuries have added about another 1,632 acres. The saltings of the Essex coast are built up of silt washed down to the sea by rivers and then thrown back on the shore by the tide. Salt water vegetation then gradually establishes itself on the deposits and the soft mud develops into saltings. On the ebb tide further particles carried in the sea are trapped by the plants. These processes continue until only the very highest spring tides are able to immerse the saltings. At this stage the vegetation is well established and gradually becomes good pasture, rich in iodine and mineral salts, on which sheep, in particular, thrive. The saltings are then ready to be 'inned' or 'reclaimed', and a sea wall is constructed to keep out the sea altogether. Rain water washes the salt, with which the newly enclosed marshes are saturated, downwards, until the surface of the marsh becomes 'fresh' when the salt-water plants are replaced by fresh-water plants and the alluvial top soil becomes highly fertile. This process has been almost entirely limited to those shores of Foulness bordered by the Thames, for the ebb tide in the rivers Crouch and Roach runs too swiftly for any appreciable deposits to take place. The coastal marshlands are easily distinguished from the rest of the county by the notable scarcity of trees and other deep-rooting plants, for, not many feet below the fertile surface the marsh remains impregnated with salt; and the fields are not bordered by hedgerows and trees, but by drainage ditches to carry away surface water.

While the 'inned' saltings become highly fertile arable land, such gain is not made without the cost of a continual threat of inundation by the sea, for as the marsh dries out it shrinks, and tends to settle behind the sea wall at a lower level than the saltings outside. Its vulnerability is thereby increased should the wall fail. Thus sea walls have been built at Foulness for two distinct purposes; to safeguard the 'original' island and to 'inn' saltings.

The first 'inning' took place at the eastern end of the island at some time before about 1420, when the marsh called New Wick, comprising 220 acres, was taken in. While the whole island as it existed at the time of the Domesday Survey can be assigned to mainland parishes[22] (the result of the pre-Domesday sub-division), New Wick remained extra-parochial until Foulness became a rectory in 1545 or 1547.[23] It is first mentioned in the manor bailiff's accounts for c.1420, and again in 1424, and formed part of the demense of the manor.

The next intake occured between the years 1424 and 1486[24], when about 358 acres were 'inned', at the eastern end of the island, and became known as Arundel Marsh. Like New Wick it was extra-parochial and formed part of the demesne of the manor.

As Miss H. E. P. Grieve has shown,[25] the sixteenth century was marked by a number of catastrophic tides, and men were more likely to have been pre-occupied with maintaining existing defences than to have been making any further intakes, and on Foulness no further additions were made until Ridge Marsh was 'inned' in the seventeenth century. It comprised about 170 acres at the eastern end of the island and was taken in sometime during the period 1620 to 1662. The first mention of it occurs in a survey of the Foulness possessions of Charles Rich, Earl of Warwick, dated 1662[26] where it is described only as marsh, in contrast to the remainder[27] which is described a 'Farm and marsh ground'. No mention of it was made in the inquisition *post mortem* of the estate of Robert Rich, 1620.[28] In 1688 it was described as a 'New-inned Marsh'.[29]

There was considerable activity during the years 1687–88, no doubt a consequence of the recent change in ownership of the manor of Foulness, it having been acquired in 1678 by Daniel Finch, Earl of Nottingham.[30] On the south side of the island 53 acres of New House Marsh,[31] 53 acres at East Wick Marsh and 37 acres at Priestwood Marsh were 'inned', while on the north side 51 acres at Nazewick and 65 acres at Monkton Barns were taken in and is the only 'inning' known to have taken place on that shore. Archaeological evidence leaves little doubt that about 44 acres were taken in on the south shore at Rugwood Marsh at the same time, but since it did not form part of Daniel Finch's estate no mention is made in his survey of 1688.[32]

No further inning took place until 1801 when East and West Newlands, an area of some 330 acres, were taken in at a cost of between £1,600 and £1,700. Like earlier intakes, the 'Newlands' became part of the manor of Foulness and in 1813 Arthur Young wrote of this intake:

> . . . three hundred and thirty acres were taken in by his Lordship's [Finch's] encouragement, by two of his tenants, Messrs. John Knapping of Shoebury, and Bannister; the bank cost between 16 and 1700l. None of it has yet been ploughed: I examined the herbage, and found it greatly advanced, and very good; with white clover coming apace, and a scattering of dwarf poa [meadow-grass], and spotted trefoil, with many other grasses that promise to do well. They have it rent free for twenty-one years. It was begun in April 1801, and finished in September.[33]

The last intake of all took place in 1833 when the whole of the saltings lying off the south shore, a total of some 251 acres, and belonging to eight farms, were 'inned'.[34]

At the present time the saltings off the south shore rarely extend more than about 100 yards from the sea wall, and are decreasing in area fairly rapidly. Off Foulness Point, however, they continue to build up. The erosion of the saltings on the south side is a new phenomenon and the cause is uncertain. It may be that the rate and force of the tidal flow of the Thames has increased

29

considerably, or that the rate at which the land is sinking relative to sea level has also increased sharply. It is certainly a question which would repay careful examination by experts.

For 1,000 years at least the special danger confronting Essex men has been the exceptionally high and vicious tide – a problem to which there may never be an absolute solution; but all the time there have been two constant, disturbing factors – the sinking of the land and the rising of the level of the sea due to the gradual melting of the polar ice caps.

It is only in recent years that the causes of the phenomenally high and disastrous tides have been fully understood. In 1919 the Liverpool Observation and Tidal Institute was formed and research carried out in its Meteorological Office showed that as a result of disturbances of sea level caused by the weather the height of the observed tide rarely coincided with that predicted. After the floods of January 1928 the Institute began to concentrate on the study of North Sea storm surges, based on tidal obervations at Southend, and it soon became apparent that the evil genius which caused the ever-recurring 'highest tide that was ever known' was the 'storm surge'. These 'surges' are caused by the drag of the wind on the surface of the sea which piles up and sets in motion a volume of water, independently of the tide. The volume of water so affected depends on the strength, direction and duration of the wind. So far as flood risk is concerned, the significant factor is the time relationship between the peak of the surge and the high tide. When the peak of the surge occurs at low tide it is harmless, but when it coincides at or near high water during spring tides it can have disastrous results, depending on its direction and strength.

Since the Essex coast is steadily sinking relative to sea level,[35] the 'highest tide that was ever known' has tended to become higher and more deadly with the passing of the centuries. The first recorded flooding on the Essex coast occurred in A.D. 31 and the *Anglo Saxon Chronicle* records a disastrous tide in November 1099.[36] It would be impossible to list every subsequent 'great tide' within the confines of this book, and the events described below are merely selective.

It would appear that the 12th, 13th and 14th centuries was a period subjected to a series of great storms, and it was the resultant anxiety that before the end of the 13th century began the issue of temporary commissions of walls and ditches (*de Walliis et Fossatis*).[37] Matthew Paris, the St. Albans Chronicler of the events of his own day, described vividly a disastrous tide flood which occurred on 12 November 1236. He wrote

> Then on the morrow of St. Martin [12 Nov.] and within the octave of the same there burst in astonishing floods of the sea, by night, suddenly, and most mightily wind resounded, with great and unusual sea and river floods together, which, especially in maritime places, deprived all ports of ships, tearing away their anchors, drowned a multitude of men, destroying flocks of sheep and herds of cattle, plucked out trees by the roots, overturned dwellings, dispersed beaches. And the ocean rose flowing with increase for two days and one night in between, which is unheard of; nor was there, as by usual custom, ebb and flow, the most mighty violence of the contrary winds, as it is laid, preventing. Then were seen the unburied bodies of the drowned, lying in sea caves by the sea shore, so that at Wisbech and in neighbouring townships, and so by the sea shore and coast, countless men perished, so that in one township, not populous, about a hundred bodies were committed in one day to mournful burial.[38]

The 'most mighty wind' on this occasion caused a surge so great that the ebb tides were overridden and the sea continued to rise for 'two days and one night in between', causing tremendous destruction and fearful loss of human life. In the second half of the fourteenth century there was a succession of calamitous tides; the winter of 1376–77 was especially bad and between February and May 1377 commissions 'of walls and ditches' were enrolled for Yorkshire, Lincolnshire, the Wash area, Norfolk and Essex, suggesting that the whole of the east coast had been devastated.[39] One of the landowners to suffer heavy loss was Barking Abbey whose estates bordered the Thames. In the summer the Abbess was forced to petition the King to be excused certain feudal obligations, because

> by flooding of the Thames they have lost great part of the profit of their possessions at Berkying and elsewhere in Essex, and have spent and are spending great part of their goods in repair of dykes broken, clearance of blocked ditches and thrusting back the water there, wherefore they may not bear the charge.[40]

On the whole the fifteenth century seems to have escaped any disasters of the magnitude of those mentioned above, but in the second half of the sixteenth century there was once again a series of 'great tides'. At the end of December 1551 two 'gret tydes' are mentioned in the Harwich churchwardens' accounts and the young King Edward VI, in a letter dated 25 January 1552 to Barnaby FitzPatrick, a Gentleman of the Privy Chamber, wrote

> Of late there hath bene such a tide heire as hath overflowen al medowes and marshes. All th'Isle of Dogges, al Plumsted marshe, al Sheppey, Foulnes in Essex, and al the sea cost was quite drowned. We here that it hath done no lesse harm in Flandres, Holland and Zellaund, but much more. For townes and cities have ben their drouned.[41]

Other serious flooding occurred in September 1564,[42] December 1565[43] and October 1570[44]. It was no doubt the result of this series of disasters which led William Camden to describe the islands of the south-east Essex archipelago as

> carrying a pleasant greene hewe, but by occasion of inundations, growne to be morish and fenny, among which these two bee of greatest name, Wallot [Wallasea] and Fouleness. . . .[45]

Foulness, and, it would seem, the whole of the Essex coast, was spared any general catastrophe during the seventeenth century. There was flooding in 1663[46] and again late in 1690, but it would appear that only the latter was serious enough to defeat the sea defences of Foulness, and was described as 'An extraordinary Spring Tyde'.[47]

The next 'outragious tide' which had a really serious effect on Foulness was that of 16 February 1736. Nathanial Salmon, in his *History of Essex* describes it as doing 'much mischief on the coast of Essex', being 'occasioned by a strong north-west wind at the time of full moon; the violence of the tide broke down the sea walls, drowned several thousands of sheep, with a large quantity of other cattle.'[48] Another account relates that

> A general inundation cover'd all the marshes and lowlands in Kent, Essex, Suffolk, Norfolk and Lincolnshire, and some thousands of cattle were destroy'd, with several of their owners in endeavouring to save them. The tide being brought in by a strong wind at N.W. was the highest of any for 135 years past . . . The little isles of Candy [Canvey] and Fowlnesse, on the coast of Essex, were quite under water, not a hoof was saved thereon, and the inhabitants were taken from the upper part of their houses into boats.[49]

Although intermittent flooding continued in other parts of the country Foulness appears to have escaped a further disaster for the next 160 years. The Commission of Sewers for Foulness, which was formed in 1800[50], carried out its duties conscientiously and its efforts were rewarded for almost a century. But even the excellent sea-walls of Foulness could not protect the island on 'Black Monday', 29 November, 1897. A gale-force north wind coincided with a spring tide, with the result that between 30,000 and 35,000 acres of land in Essex went under water, but without loss of human life. All of the 'inned' land on Foulness except New Wick – or about one-third of the total – was submerged, but miraculously the original medieval walls, known as 'counter-walls' stood up to the pressure and so saved the rest of the island, including the hamlet of Church End.[51] The island's walls were constructed 12 inches higher than before as a result of the recommendations of a consultant engineer called in by the Commissioners.[52] After the flood Mr. T. S. Dymond, staff chemist of the Essex Technical Instruction Committee, made a special investigation into the effect of sea water flooding on the land, and had this to say of Foulness:

> The inundation lasted on different portions from one to six days. After the water subsided the ground was found to be covered with dead worms, which seagulls devoured. At first it was thought that the injury would be confined to the then growing crops, for the soil, when afterwards ploughed, was found to be in a very workable condition, the texture having apparently been improved by the salt water. As soon as rain had washed out the salt from the surface soil, however, the condition speedily deteriorated, and the soil finally became so difficult to work and so hard and caked in dry weather, that proper aeration and root action were inhibited.[53]

But by 1907, when the Essex Field Club made an excursion to the island, things had changed for the better and the honorary secretary reported that

> On the pieces of permanent grassland crossed by the Club, clover, which was destroyed by salt water, has reappeared. The texture of the soil seems to have got back almost to its original condition, partly perhaps, because worms have again become abundant. A difference in the cropping is noticeable, for while the effect of the salt water lasted it was important to cultivate as cheaply as possible, and a good deal of land was in consequence laid down with lucerne. Both lucerne and other crops appear to be doing well. But there is one legacy which the flood has bequeathed to the islanders – weeds. For when the soil was in such a condition that crops could not grow, the land was left a prey to colts-foot and to twitch, the latter being a grass which has always been abundant on the ditch banks of the island in spite of the brackish water which the ditches contain.[54]

Foulness was flooded for up to six days in 1897, and ten years after the disaster the island had not recovered but was only making 'great progress' towards recovery. The twentieth century opened badly; there was further flooding on the Essex coast on 28 November 1901, October and November 1903, 30 December 1904, New Year 1905, and March 1906. Foulness escaped disaster on each of these occasions with a narrow margin of safety.

On Friday night, 6–7 January 1928 a spring tide coincided with a north-westerly gale; fourteen people were drowned in basements in Westminster, Hammersmith and Fulham and the *Essex Chronicle* described the tide as 'the highest flood tide within living memory'. Huge areas of the Essex coastal marshlands went under water, causing immense damage to agriculture and industry. This tide was more than a foot higher than that of 1897,[55] but again Foulness escaped serious flooding.

CHAPTER VI

THE GREAT TIDE[1]

On the night of 31 January–1 February 1953 the worst flooding ever known occurred on the low-lying coastal areas of Holland and eastern England which front the North Sea. As in the case of all previous flooding it was caused by severe gale-force northerly winds, gusting to hurricane-force, coinciding with a spring tide, which resulted in the greatest 'surge' ever recorded. The predicted height for high water at Southend which was due at 1.30 a.m., 1 February, was 8.7 feet above mean sea level, but when the tide ceased flowing at 1.30 a.m. it had risen 15.7 feet above mean sea level – 7 feet higher than predicted and 3½ feet above danger level.

The result was disastrous. In Essex alone the sea broke into 12,356 homes, 119 human lives were lost as a result and 21,000 people were made homeless. The sea flooded 49,000 acres (more than 76 square miles), 41,760 of which were agricultural, and the rest industrial and residential.

During 1951–52 the sea walls at Foulness were strengthened and raised to a height of 16½ feet above mean sea level by the War Department. The island was therefore one of the best protected areas of the Essex coast and the overtopping of the walls was not caused by the height of the tide, but by vicious waves raised by the wind. This wave action led to so much overtopping, scouring of the unprotected landward side of the walls, slipping and breaching, at two points on the island (on Thames-side from Rugwood Head to Asplins Head and on Crouch-side for about a mile westwards from Foulness Point) that enough water was let in to reduce the island, where the average ground level is only 7 feet above mean sea level and in places as little as 3 feet, to 'an abandoned desolation of wind-swept water unequalled anywhere in the county'.

From about 2 a.m. on 1 February the sea poured into Foulness and by 6 a.m. the island and its inhabitants were completely cut off from the mainland, with the neighbouring islands submerged and the telephone link and gas and electricity supplies broken. During that Sunday all rescue attempts to reach Foulness failed and anxiety on the mainland for its inhabitants mounted. What it was like on Foulness that Sunday, as it dragged on without sign of rescue, was described by the farmer at Rugwood.

> When daylight came all we could see was one vast expanse of water, with only the tops of gates, and a few trees and haystacks. The wind was still very strong and the weather was very cold. From the bedroom windows we could see the gaps in the sea wall where the water had broken through. Floating about on the water were bales of hay and straw, timber, chicken houses, and even stacks of straw.
>
> As I could not get to the yards where the animals were, I called to my foreman, who lived just by the yards. As he could not hear anything of them he looked from a bedroom window and saw that the eighteen cattle in one yard were drowned.
>
> I then saw my horseman, who had waded from the village along the main road, and had tried to get across to where the horses were in their stable. The water was too deep and he was forced to turn back, very distressed.
>
> I then decided to go indoors and change my clothes, as it was very cold.
>
> There was no electricity nor water supply on the island, but we were fortunate in having a hot water tank from which we could draw, also Calor gas, which was not affected by the flood water, so we were able to get hot meals.
>
> At the time we were completely isolated, but in the village [Church End] . . . the people helped each other as much as possible. Most of the men had rubber thigh-boots, and we were able to wade from house to house. Fires were lit in

bedrooms, and where no coal or wood was available children's toys, old gramo-phone records, etc., were used for fuel. People in whose homes the water was deepest were, where possible, taken into other houses. The depth of water varied considerably over the island at first . . . but with the second tide more water rushed through the broken walls, it became deeper than before, and remained in many places for more than three weeks.

All day Sunday we could only watch from the bedroom windows to see how the animals were faring. They travelled about the fields, swimming from one place to another. Several were drowned in the deep water – particularly sheep. Others became entangled in fences. Nothing could be seen of any poultry, as they were still in the houses, which had either been tipped over, or were floating about. As for the birds and wild animals – partridges and pheasants were in trees and on stacks – rabbits were floating about on pieces of timber, and even up trees.

Inside the house we splashed about in rubber boots, the womenfolk (my wife and my mother) getting meals and hot drinks in the flooded kitchen. One of the chief difficulties was keeping our children out of the water, but we did manage to keep them upstairs.

As the evening came it was a very miserable sight. The water made the house so cold, we could only keep a very small fire to save fuel, and as we sat by the light of candles listening to the lapping of the water round the house, and the cries of the animals, we wondered what the morrow would bring.

Throughout that Sunday plans were laid by the Army and civilian services, including Southend lifeboat, to rescue the inhabitants early the following day, and reception centres were prepared for them in the Royal Corinthian Yacht Club at Burnham, and at the village hall at Great Wakering. The rescue operation which followed was a Dunkirk evacuation in miniature, but this time the enemy was the sea. During Monday little groups of people, chilled with cold, hungry and exhausted after their ordeal, arrived at Burnham, and Great Wakering where the villages took them into their homes; they had been rescued by an amazing assortment of craft, including fishermen in their rowing boats, an Army DUKW, the Southend lifeboat and a barge. On that Monday a total of 335 people were evacuated from the island. Only 30 men remained, farmers and farmworkers who refused to leave their animals, but all but six of these were compulsorily taken off the following day for their own safety. Miraculously, only two people lost their lives.

With the inhabitants evacuated, there remained the problem of rescuing the farm stock and the enormous task of rebuilding the sea defences. Time was short for the animals were cold, hungry, thirsty and frightened, and within a fortnight spring tides would again reach their peak, accompanying the new moon of 14 February.

Most of the animals were reported to be alive, but dispersed in small groups all over the island, many of them standing up to their bellies in water. The first and most difficult task was to round them up and get them to Church End, preferably in the churchyard, where they could be tended more easily than in their isolated positions. All attempts at this operation failed on Monday 2 February through lack of suitable boats. A further difficulty was that each expedition of farmers and farm workers, R.S.P.C.A. officials and soldiers was ruled by the tide, because the road was still blocked and the only way was across the sands to Fisherman's Head.

On Wednesday 4 February a convoy of DUKWs and four-wheel-drive three-ton lorries left before dawn carrying food and water for the animals. Once on the island the expedition split into two parties which during the day herded together as many animals as they could on higher ground. Most were taken to the churchyard, where they were fed and watered. On 5 February as many animals as possible were moved along the military road to Newhouse Farm, near Fisherman's Head, ready for evacuation the following day. Before dawn on the 6th, a fleet of twenty-four hauliers' cattle lorries drove along the Broomway, accompanied by the divisional veterinary surgeon who was in charge of loading and during that morning most of the animals were evacuated. Some lorries even managed to make the journey twice in the interval of one low water. By the following day, Saturday, the evacuation of the animals was completed, with the exception of sixteen dairy cows at Monkton Barns which were taken off by barge on Sunday.

During the course of these operations about 40 beasts which were too weak to be moved had to be destroyed, and a number of others were drowned. In addition, 700 sheep and 249 pigs died before they could be rescued. Yet the number of livestock evacuated can only be described as remarkable, and amounted to:

400 Cattle	6 Lambs	2 Dogs
14 Calves	3 Pigs	10 Rabbits
28 Horses	670 Chickens	4 Budgerigars
72 Sheep	100 Ducks	16 Dairy Cows

The bare chronology of this rescue operation conveys nothing of the desperate nature of the undertaking. Only the personal accounts of those taking part can give a true picture of the events of those few dreadful days. The farmer at Rugwood wrote of the operations on Tuesday and Wednesday

> There were little groups of sheep – standing on high ground or on floating bales of straw. On arriving at the first group, consisting of three sheep, we found they were standing on the dead bodies of about 50 drowned sheep. We put the three in the rowing boat, and then rowed back to the DUKW and transferred the sheep on to it.
>
> When we arrived at the next group, which were in a shed with some hay, we discovered a ewe with twin lambs; she had her leg broken by stampeding cattle. We transferred these with five more sheep to the DUKW, and the mother ewe was destroyed by the R.S.P.C.A. We carried on for the remainder of that day rescuing what sheep we could, until 4 o'clock when we had to join the convoy across the sands before the tide covered the track.
>
> Of the many problems of the evacuation the greatest was the cattle, as they were without food or water, and became very restless in their unsuccessful search for food. They came into contact with barbed wire fences, some were caught on these and drowned, others managed to get through.
>
> After releasing the 92 cattle from the yards [at Rugwood] they all made for the same direction – and arrived at the buildings surrounding the farm house. Several were drowned on the way. Having the cattle together, we hoped to transfer them to the other end of the island by means of the main road, but they made straight for the evergreens in the garden, and trod everything down that was in their way. They remained there for that day.
>
> When we arrived on the island the next day we came straight to the farmyards hoping to get the cattle on the road. We tried several methods; one was to put hay in our rowing boat hoping they would follow it. This they did, but we had to jump out of the boat as the cattle were trying to get in after the hay. We then tried another method. This time we roped one of the strongest bullocks to the DUKW and tried to tow it out of the yard, hoping the rest would follow. This attempt failed as we had to cut the bullock loose or it would have drowned. Having no success then with my own cattle, we went across to my neighbour's farm [Priestwood], with the help of two of his men who were on horseback we managed to drive his cattle down the main road to the churchyard which was one of the highest places. We used this as a corral to feed and water them.

The work was carried out under appalling conditions. Each day the rescue parties left Shoebury before daylight and returned home after dark. The gunner-major in charge of the convoys reported:

> It was not uncommon for the men to work throughout the day soaked to the skin despite the fact they had been provided by the military with rubber thigh boots. Unexpected ditches and trip wires were usually the cause. But we were fortunate in the weather which, though cold, was sunny and bright, and the men were generally working so hard and kept so busy that they had not time in which to worry about their own physical condition.
>
> I must pay special tribute to the farm workers, who performed prodigious feats in handling terrified animals. Their good humour I have never seen surpassed anywhere.

Of all the feats performed by farmers, and farmworkers, troops and R.S.P.C.A. inspectors in those few days, the extrication of ninety-odd head of cattle from the farmyard at Rugwood at the third attempt was, perhaps, the most outstanding. Had this last attempt, which took place on Thursday, failed, there would have been no alternative but to destroy the whole herd. One of the R.S.P.C.A. inspectors described how two Priestwood men on horseback, and farmers, farmworkers, and inspectors with sticks, formed up behind the cattle.

> A 'Duck' with hay on board, which was thrown on to the water to tempt the cattle, was standing by, and as a beast caught by the ropes around the horns was slowly hauled away from the others, the men on the 'Duck' yelled their heads off, whilst we beat and screamed at them from behind. For fifteen minutes they did not move, and then we took our killers out and fired into the air, and slowly they moved, only to stop a after a few yards; some returned behind us, others drifted into sheds on the way, but as we followed them up, slowly the depths of water rose and we were in it up to our stomachs, our feet bitterly cold: still we all surged on, not daring to give up the pursuit, and then the yelling was broken by cheers as the first beast reached the road, two or three feet beneath the water, and the beasts were on their way to safety. We turned to each other and embraced ourselves; I celebrated by firing a volley into the air. This in the opinion of all the rescue workers was the greatest rescue of the whole flood on Foulness Island.

At the same time as the animals were being taken off the island the War Department's efforts to secure the sea walls before the next spring tides were getting into full swing. Three Royal Naval minesweepers, the *Rinaldo*, *Cheerful* and *Cockatrice*, were moored off Foulness Point and accommodated the Army personnel working on the walls. By 9 February 300 soldiers and 70 sailors were engaged in this work. By the 11th the number of men had increased to 400 soldiers and 100 sailors, but still more were needed to secure the walls before the spring tides reached their peak on the 16th. On the 14th a serious setback took place at Shelford Creek, which was inacessible except

> by foot along the top of the sea wall from the main road, a distance of 1,500 yards, and all tools, sandbags, etc., had to be carried along this route.
>
> In order to obtain a foundation for the final closing of the breach 2 pontoons had been supplied but the only available materials for filling the sandbags was the wet mud from the saltings.
>
> On Saturday 14th February the time had come to seal this breach finally. Work was carried out during the whole of the morning without a break in order to beat the tide, but I had not sufficient men to do the job, and when the tide came in, it proved to be 1½ feet higher than predicted, and we had the mortification of watching the results of our labours washed away in a few moments.

But on the 15th and 16th the walls held, and the worst was over for the tides had reached their peak and would not again reach that level for a fortnight. The people of Foulness were not allowed back for six weeks. On the 10th, 11th and 12th March the War Department Land Agent carried out a survey, but did not advise re-occupation until 19 March because of the spring tides due on the 14th and 15th. In the meantime the houses were being inspected to see if they were fit to live in, and many people travelled to the island each day to clean and scrub. About 80 of the 114 families who lived on the island returned on 19 March.

But this was only the beginning; it was to be many months, even years, before everything was back to normal. The bodies of hundreds of dead animals which were discovered as the water receded had to be removed; gates, ladders, stack covers, barrels of oil, and hundreds of bales of hay and straw, which were found scattered over the island, all had to be returned to their rightful owners; homes had to be redecorated. Most important of all, it was to be several years before the ill-effects on the soil of the salt water saturation were completely eliminated and the island restored to its former agricultural prosperity. As terrible as it was, the disaster might have been worse, for as Miss Grieve has shown:

> The storm surge might have occurred when heavy rainfall had already swollen the Essex rivers; it might have been superimposed upon spring tides with a higher predicted range; its peak might have coincided more closely with the predicted time of high water; and the wind might have veered at the critical moment to the north-east . . . and increased in Essex wave action on the open coast.

And there is little that the people of Foulness, or anywhere else in the low-lying coastal regions, can do except protect themselves with higher and stronger defences. It is only a matter of time before another tide rises even higher than the 'Great Tide' and only then will it be known whether the coastal defences are sufficiently strong to cope with it.

CHAPTER VII

MISCELLANY

Historians and chroniclers from the 16th to the 19th century when writing about Foulness have always agreed on one thing – that it produced unhealthiness in man. Before 1830 there was no regular supply of fresh water on the island,[1] which, coupled with its low-lying position, subject to continual dampness and occasional floods, and its position exposed to biting east winds, led to the popular, and not inaccurate, opinion of Foulness as a place where one would not live if it could be avoided. In the eighteenth century few of the tenant farmers resided on the island,[2] which was inhabited by the hardy descendants of sixteenth-century peasantry and fishermen,[3] and descendants of Dutch settlers of the seventeenth century, and an assortment of persons such as escaped criminals and other runaways from justice, who were usually known by nickname only.[4] Until about the middle of the nineteenth century the population was not only predominantly male,[5] but also particularly rough, lawless and 'offensive to decency'.[6] A group of papers preserved among the Essex Quarter Sessions dealing with the wreck on the Foulness Sands in March 1775 of the collier-brig *Sea Flower*, bound from Sunderland to London with a cargo of coal, leave little doubt that Foulness men were engaged in deliberate wrecking at that time.[7] In the early nineteenth century the island was famous for its bare-fist fighters, and many of the bloody encounters took place in the church yard and what is now the garden in front of the 'George and Dragon' public house.[8] The most celebrated of the Foulness fighters was John Bennewith, the 'Foulness Champion', and a man of great muscular development, who began his pugilistic career in 1810.[9] His mother was the owner of the 'George and Dragon'.

By the middle of the nineteenth century this atmosphere of unhealthiness, lawlessness and violence was becoming a thing of the past. The discovery of a regular supply of fresh water[10] did much to improve conditions on the island, for both man and beast, so much so that in 1867 Benton wrote:

> Ague is now seldom heard of. The health of the inhabitants is probably better than those in the uplands, and the island is capable of being made one of the most salubrious spots in the country.[11]

And of the inhabitants themselves he had this to say:

> . . . nowadays, thanks partly to the supervision of police and improved tone of morals, the spread of education, a greater care for their souls by their minister, and the spread of religious principles, Foulness is not behind the parishes of the mainland in morality. Crime is now more rarely heard of, and a resident policeman is considered unnecessary.[12]

The Minister referred to was the Reverend Harvey Vachell who was appointed to the living in 1844 and who 'set about reforming the manners and morals of the inhabitants, who were exceedingly rough and ignorant . . .'[13] It is an interesting fact, and a praiseworthy one for the people of Foulness, that a resident policeman is still considered unnecessary. Another factor which helped to improve conditions on the island was the inheritance of the Finch estates[14] in 1826 by George Finch Esq. He was a kind, considerate and 'improving' landlord, much liked by his tenantry, who in 1837 presented him with a portrait of himself by Samuel Laurence.[15] In 1846 the first provision for education on the island was made when a Church of England school was opened. It was designed to accommodate 120 children, and one master, Clement Cater, was appointed.[16] While these improvements were taking place, the annual fair, which was held opposite the 'King's Head' at Courts End on 10 July, was discontinued about 1850 because of disorderliness.[17]

During the Middle Ages the island's resident population had probably consisted of only a few shepherds. In 1424 there were five shepherds within the manor looking after the sheep and cattle and it is probable that some of the marshes not forming part of the manor also had a shepherd. The only buildings within the manor in 1424 were the 'grange' and three fishermen's workshops erected on sea-walls.[18] It is unlikely that the fishermen were resident on the island.[19] In the sixteenth century the population expanded rapidly; the reasons are not easy to give, partly because of the lack of documentary evidence, but it can probably be associated with the final decline of the manorial agricultural system and the leasing of the demesne lands to tenant farmers. Since the dairy industry was already in decline[20] it is reasonable to assume that the proportion of land devoted to crop growing was increasing, a change which would result in the necessity for a much larger labour force. The seventeenth century witnessed a substantial influx of Dutch settlers,[21] possibly to be associated with the 'innings' which took place during that century.[22] In the nineteenth century the island's population rose steadily until the 1870s when a peak of about 750 persons was achieved, after which time it began to decline, and continued a downward trend until the present-day figure of about 250 inhabitants[23] was reached. The following table is based on the ten-yearly census returns of England and Wales, which began in 1801.

Date	Total Population	Male Population	Female Population	Number of Inhabited Houses	Number of Uninhabited Houses
1801	396	251	145	43	nil
1811	450	309	141	46	nil
1821	565	367	198	not given	not given
1831	630	424	206	78	1
1841	674	437	237	100	3
1851	640	399	241	109	nil
1861	681	424	257	109	nil
1871	754	447	307	127	2
1881	706	415	291	114	7
1891	676	402	274	119	7
1901	537	331	206	96	17
1911	479	270	209	not given	not given
1921	460	263	197	96	nil
1931	414	233	181	112	nil
1951	371	182	189	120[24]	not given
1961	316	165	151	104[24]	not given

A number of other interesting factors arise from the census returns. During the years when so many improvements were being made in the quality and conditions of life on Foulness, the female population increased markedly in proportion to the male population; in 1831 there were 424 males and 206 females, but in 1861 the male figure remained at 424 while the number of females had increased to 257, while in the next decade the male population increased by 23 and the female population by 50. A number of explanations may be offered for the proportionately heavy male population, which was also to be found on neighbouring mainland parishes, thought not to so marked a degree, while in England and Wales as a whole, during the period discussed, there was (and still is) a small excess of females. In the early decades of the nineteenth century in particular, Foulness harboured large numbers of men seeking to escape justice, who were unlikely to bring families with them to the island, while most of the tenant farmers, who were likely to have large, balanced families, chose not to live on the island.[25] The parish was almost wholly agricultural; as a result there was employment more suitable to male than female labour, and there can be little doubt that large numbers of females left the island to enter domestic service, particularly in London. In 1801 the number of persons employed in agriculture amounted to 229, while only 17 were engaged in trade, manufacture or handicrafts, and in 1831 there were 92 families on the island, of which 77 were engaged in agriculture and only 10 in trade or manufacture.

In April 1969 the population of Foulness and Havengore Islands was 241, of which 128 were males and 113 were females. Forty-four were aged 16 and under, 163 were between 17 and 64, and 34 were aged 65 or over. Of the working population 36 per cent were engaged in agriculture, 39 per cent were employed by the government (Ministry of Defence) and 25 per cent were in other occupations. The population of Foulness (excluding the families of forces personnel) is perhaps unique in south-east England, for most of the inhabitants are a closely related family. An examination of the parish registers has revealed that nearly all the families have lived on the island for several generations at least, and the oldest extant family, that of Cripps,[26] is related to almost all the other families in varying degrees.[27]

It is clear from the census returns at the beginning of the nineteenth century that housing conditions on the island were appalling,[28] with 396 people living in 43 houses, or almost nine people per dwelling, most of which were small cottages. The position was even worse in 1811 when 450 people shared 46 houses, almost 10 people per dwelling. In 1826 George Finch became the owner of the greater part of the island, and within a few years there was a marked improvement, for in 1831 there were 78 houses inhabited by 630 people, just over eight per dwelling, half of which were newly built of brick. The building of new houses continued steadily over the next twenty years so that in 1841 there were 100 houses inhabited by 674 persons, and in 1851 109 houses inhabited by 640 persons, less than 6 persons per dwelling. Much of this early-Victorian building still remains, and includes the school and church, as well as numerous cottages and small houses.

Despite a rapidly increasing population and the marked predominance of males, there was a labour shortage in the mid-nineteenth century. Benton commented on this problem, as well as on the system of 'lookers' which[29] had been in operation for at least a century, and probably much longer.

> One drawback to farming in Foulness is the scarcity of labour, and consequently its dearness. This falls upon the master, as the lookers enjoy the privilege of retailing goods to the men, which they do at higher rates than if regular shops were established. Some farmers have been known to pursue this plan themselves, a sort of truck system prevailing, and pork and old sows of sixty stone and upwards have been purchased for the labourers. The latter, like their brethren on the mainland, are now more fastidious as to their diet. The dearness of labour is increased by the improvident habits of many, the employers not having sufficient control over them so as to prevent their spending considerable time in drinking, frequently in hay and other busy seasons.[30]

Benton's comments about drinking are not without good foundation. The parish registers record among the burials for 1787–98 five persons who, according to Coroner's inquests, 'died of excessive drinking.'[31]

Until about the beginning of this century the labourers' staple food had been fish, trapped on the extensive off-shore sands in kiddles or weirs, and stewed in large cauldrons. In 1813 Arthur Young wrote of these fish stews:

> The salt water stews for various sorts of sea fish in Foulness Island, are well contrived, and answer the purpose completely. The fish are caught in weirs, on the extensive sands which extend several miles on the coast, and deposited when plentiful in these stews, where they drag for them with a small net, as in a fresh water stew.[32]

Another problem, and one which faced all the inhabitants, was difficulty of access from the mainland. The roads on the island were in 'a state of nature'[33] but this was a minor inconvenience compared with that which confronted those wishing to travel between the mainland of Rochford Hundred and the island, and the problem was not overcome until 1922 when the military road from Great Wakering was opened. Until that time access was by ferry, or at low water from Wakering Stairs along the Broomway. The Broomway is an ancient trackway which runs for a distance of six miles across the Maplin Sands, following the contour of the land about a quarter of a mile from the shore. At several points, branches, called 'headways', which formerly served local farms, lead to the shore. The track derives its name from the hundreds of bunches of small poles or twigs buried in the sand and shaped like inverted besoms (fire-brooms) which marked the seaward side of the track. Since 1922 it has gradually fallen into disuse and is now only used by Ministry of Defence vehicles for recovering shells and other missiles fired on to the Maplin Sands from the Shoebury and Foulness batteries. When it was in regular use the Broomway must surely have been the most dangerous road in England, for the Maplins, a continuation of the Foulness Sands, are a vast area of almost level sand, and once the sea has reached that level, miles out, it floods over the rest like a mill race. At the same time as the sea has been flowing in from the seaward side, it has also been flowing into the numerous creeks along that part of the coast from the Crouch and Roach side, and about the time the seaward tide reaches the Broomway, the shoreward one also touches it, and in the conflict as to which shall hold sway swirling zones and miniature whirlpools are formed. In misty weather it is impossible to judge where the shore is from the direction of the tide and many unfortunate travellers have struggled out to sea to meet their deaths in the belief that, as it was ostensibly 'coming in' they were approaching the shore, and in the parish registers of burials there are numerous mentions of parishioners and strangers found drowned.[34]

In the mid-nineteenth century there were three ferries, to Burnham, Wallasea Island and Potton Island.[35] The island had been served by ferries for centuries, and the bailiffs' accounts for c.1420, 1424 and 1486 mention such a boat bringing fresh water from the mainland.[36] Yet the island's maritime position, which has caused so much inconvenience to human travellers, was also, until the coming of the internal combustion engine, a source of economic strength, for as Mr. Arthur Brown has shown in his *Essex at Work, 1700–1815*

> When farms near the coast were advertised, proximity to water transport was a major recommendation. . . . Even farmers living inland found it economical to send produce to London through the nearest port or quay . . . [and] Scores of minor loading places enjoyed an often busy trade, due to the high cost of road transport.[37]

Foulness is not rich in ancient buildings. The church (which has already been described)[38] built in 1850–52, the Church of England school and the rectory,[39] both built in 1846, are all typical examples of early Victorian brick building. The oldest dwelling is New House Farm which dates from the mid-seventeenth century. It is timber-framed and three-storied with a gambrel roof and weather boarding, and is the only remaining building on the island which shows Dutch influence to any degree. The timber-framed and weatherboarded 'George and Dragon' public house was built about 1650, originally as three cottages,[40] but was extensively rebuilt in the first half of the nineteenth century. Priestwood farmhouse dates from about 1700 and Rugwood from about 1750, both replacing earlier buildings. They are timber-framed and weatherboarded, but neither have any particular architectural merit. Lodge Farm is a pleasant brick house of about 1810, and Old Hall, the manor house, was completely rebuilt in brick about 1850. Many interesting buildings have been demolished by the Ministry of Defence, which owns all the buildings on the island except the church, rectory, school, village hall and mission hall at Courts End. The parish post-mill, which had been built at the beginning of the nineteenth century at a cost of £536[41] and stood near the Post Office at Church End, was demolished early in the First World War,[42] and the parish poor-house, which stood half-way between Old Hall and Lodge Farm, and a 'square, pyramidical topped, wooden 'cage' or lock-up, which stood outside the church yard'[43] have both likewise disappeared.

About the middle of the seventeenth century Dutch names first appear in Foulness records. It is commonly believed on the island that the Dutch came to repair and extend embankments and reclaim land. There is probably much truth in this legend, for they appear to have first arrived at the time when Ridge Marsh was being 'inned' (1620–1662).[44] The parish registers, which unfortunately have only survived from 1695,[45] abound with names like Moorebeck, Bennewithe, Douset, Lodwick, Peroose, Damion, Vanderzee, Ballaugh and Rippengale. The Dutch influence was still so strong until the First World War that many female islanders wore Dutch costumes as normal attire. The Dutch influence in buildings has already been mentioned.

Foulness Point is designated as an area of special scientific interest under Section 23 of the National Parks and Access to the Countryside Act 1949 and this chapter would not be complete without some reference to the other inhabitants of Foulness – the wildfowl.[46] Chief among these are the Dark-breasted Brent Geese, which are winter visitors to this country from Siberia. The world population of this sub-species increased from about 16,500 in the mid-1950s to about 24,000 in late 1960, and is still increasing. One third of the world population winters in Essex, particularly around Foulness Point, where a flock of 12,500 occurred recently. The Little Tern is a summer resident in Essex between the extreme dates of 1 April and 1 November. There are seven coastal colonies of which Foulness is the most important, with up to 95 pairs, and it is one of the three largest in the British Isles. The Bartailed Godwit is present on the Essex coast throughout the year, though generally it is uncommon between late May and early August, and is chiefly a winter visitor. Its stronghold is the Foulness–Wakering area, where its numbers are increasing with concentrations typically around 500–600 birds, though this figure is frequently surpassed; for example, in September 1965 there were 3,000. Like the Brent Goose, the Oystercatcher is a winter visitor to the Essex coast. The largest flocks (2–3,000, maximum 6,000 in October 1965) are to be found at Foulness Point and its numbers are increasing.

CHAPTER VIII

FOULNESS AND THE FUTURE

This chapter deals very briefly with the possibility of a third London airport and a great dock complex being built on the Maplin and Foulness Sands. It is not the purpose of this book to present a detailed argument for or against the proposals; indeed, to do so would necessitate printing a very large volume. To those who wish to pursue this matter more deeply it is suggested that the *Papers and Proceedings of the Commission on the Third London Airport*, vol. iii, stage ii, Local Hearings Foulness (off shore), be consulted.

In 1968 the Government set up a Commission headed by The Hon. Mr. Justice Roskill to find the most suitable site for a third London airport and to investigate the timing of the need for such an airport. Preliminary investigations in 1968 produced a short-list of four potential sites of which the Maplin Sands off Foulness is one, the others being Cublington (Bucks.), Nuthampstead (Herts.) and Thurleigh (Beds.). In addition the Thames Estuary Development Company (TEDCO) is proposing a joint airport-seaport on the Maplin Sands, which could accommodate ships of up to 500,000 tons by 1990. This venture would involve this reclamation of 18,000 acres of the Maplin Sands and access to the port through the Thames Estuary would be by dredged channels. Similar proposals to those of TEDCO are being put forward by Thames Aeroport Group Ltd.

The following analysis is based on the *Papers and Proceedings* of the Commission, vol. vii, parts 1 and 2, and represents the findings of the Commission's Research Team. It also illustrates something of the complexity of the problem of choosing the most suitable site.

1. Net cost of building *airport only*

Foulness	Cublington	Nuthampstead	Thurleigh
£179m.	£184m.	£178m.	£176m.

2. *Total* net cost of building (this includes such elements as the removal of defence establishments, building road and rail links to airport, insulation of buildings against noise, loss of agricultural output, provision of airport service, etc.)

Foulness	Cublington	Nuthampstead	Thurleigh
£252.7m.	£288.8m.	£284.7m.	£288.3m.

3. But the figures in 2 above do not include 'social costs' (loss of amenities, air passengers' travelling time to airport, depreciation of property values, work journeys of airport employees, etc.). With these factors included total net costs become:

Foulness	Cublington	Nuthampstead	Thurleigh
£2,385.2m.	£2,264.6m.	£2,273.9m.	£2,266.3m.

Some factors considered by the public and popular press to be important, in fact constitute only very small costs in terms of money.

a. Wildfowl and gliding. Cost of providing alternative sanctuaries for irreplaceable wildfowl and alternative gliding facilities.

b. To provide bird-scaring devices to give safety to aircraft.

c. Bird-strike hazard from those birds which cannot be discouraged.

d. Visibility.

e. Loss of agricultural output from urbanisation.

	Foulness £	Cublington £	Nuthampstead £	Thurleigh £
a.	0.3m.	0.05m.	0.07m.	0.02m.
b.	0.136m.	0.07m.	0.07m.	0.07m.
c.	1.38m.	0.46m.	0.46m.	0.46m.
d.	1.6m.	5.0 m.	3.0m.	2.0m.
e.	4.2m.	3.1m.	7.2m.	4.6m.

(All figures are based on 1968 prices and discounted to 1975 at 10 per cent. per annum).

It is not the first time that man has planned to reclaim the Maplin Sands. In the 1850s The South Essex Estuary and Reclamation Company proposed to reclaim 30,420 acres of saltings and flats off the Essex coat, including the Maplin Sands, Foulness Sands, Ray Sand, Dengie Flats, and St Peter's Sands. The Company employed Sir John Rennie (1794–1874), a member of the famous family of nineteenth century civil engineers, to draw up the plans. A wall about 20 miles long was to run from near Wakering Stairs to just round Foulness Point, and another wall 11 miles long was to run from Holliwell Point (Burnham) to Sales Point (Bradwell-juxta-Mare). The marshes, flats and sands of the Blackwater estuary and Mersea Island were also to be extensively embanked. The plans were deposited with the Clerk of the Peace of Essex in 1851[1] and approved by Act of Parliament in 1852.[2] The Act authorised the issue of 8,000 shares at £50 and the right to borrow up to £183,000 and the work had to be completed within 14 years.

Work commenced at Sales Point where a causeway was run out for 1¼ miles and a creek dug at a cost of £3,884, but it seems that this was the limit of the work undertaken. Another Act was secured by the Company in 1866[3] but in 1868 an order in Chancery was issued that the company should wind up its affairs when £21,000 had been sunk into the adventure and £3,884 had been paid to the contractor.[4] The reasons for the failure are not absolutely clear, but probably resulted from lack of financial backing. In addition, there was very considerable opposition from local landowners.[5]

The next scheme for the reclamation of large areas of the Essex coast was that of the Metropolis Sewage and Essex Reclamation Company whose object was to reclaim the flats of Foulness and Dengie Hundred. An important feature of this Company's proposals was the construction of pipelines from London to Foulness and Dengie to carry the capital's sewage on to the areas to be reclaimed.[6] Other schemes followed in 1862, 1865 and 1879, but all came to nothing. During the period 1850–1880 all successful enclosures were on a small scale, and were carried out by the local landowners. After 1880 depression in agriculture deterred both private bodies and public companies from any further attempts at reclamation.[7]

Whether or not a great airport–seaport will be built off Foulness is, at the time of writing, unknown. For centuries, because of its peculiar geographical position and the difficulty of access it has remained a quiet backwater of the county, gently touched by time. Even the coming of the Proof and Experimental Establishment of the Ministry of Defence early this century and the opening of the military road from Great Wakering in 1922 has had little effect, for there is no general public access to the island, and it remains what it has always been, quiet, remote, and, save the occasional gunfire or detonation, utterly peaceful.

1. MEDIEVAL SEA WALL

Most of the old roads and tracks on Foulness run on top of internal (or counter) sea walls. The wall shown here, photographed from the perimeter wall at Crouch Loading, was probably constructed by the twelfth century, perhaps earlier. The land on the right is Nase Wick, part of the 'original' island, and that to the left is Arundel Marsh, 'inned' between 1424 and 1486.

2. ON THE BROOMWAY, 1907

Members of the Essex Field Club travelling on the Broomway from Fisherman's Head to Wakering Stairs in May 1907. Many unfortunate travellers have been trapped by the tide and drowned whilst taking this dangerous route across the Maplin Sands, and persons without good local knowledge should under no circumstances attempt the journey.

3. THE QUAY

The Quay on the River Roach at Monkton Barns was the landing place for the ferry from Wallasea Island and one of many places where sailing barges loaded the island's produce for the short sea passage to London. Unauthorised persons landing here are likely to be arrested by the Military.

4. OLD HALL FARMHOUSE

Old Hall farmhouse at Church End was built in the mid-nineteenth century on the site of an earlier house. It was also the manor house and courts were held here until the War Department acquired the manor in 1915. The church spire may be seen to the left of the picture.

5. RUGWOOD FARMHOUSE

The farm or marsh of Rugwood is first mentioned in 1246 and between 1483 and 1486 it was incorporated into the manor of Foulness. It is unlikely that there were any buildings, other than sheepfolds and perhaps a shepherd's shelter, before the sixteenth century, and the present timber-framed farmhouse dates from the mid-eighteenth century.

6. PRIESTWOOD FARMHOUSE

Priestwood Marsh is first mentioned in 1308, but, as in the case of all the other marshes, there was probably no farmhouse before the sixteenth century. The present house dates from about 1700, with later additions, and it has recently been heavily and somewhat insensitively restored by its owners, the Ministry of Defence.

7. THE 'GEORGE AND DRAGON'

The timber-framed and weather-boarded 'George and Dragon' at Church End was originally constructed as three cottages about 1650 and became an inn in the following century. In the first half of the nineteenth century the landlady was Mrs. Bennewith, whose son, John, was the greatest of all Foulness bare-fist fighters. Many of the bloody encounters, which continued until the incumbency of the Reverend Harvey Vachell (1844–47), took place in the garden in front of the pub. Behind the wall on the left is the churchyard.

8. PARISH CHURCH OF ST MARY

The present church of St. Mary was built in 1852 to the designs of William Hambley, replacing the first (Tudor) parish church which stood immediately to the south, and which in turn replaced the medieval chantry chapel established by Lady Joan de Bohun in 1386.

Farm or Marsh	Area reclaimed during 1687–8	Area in 1688 including land reclaimed in 1687–8 but excluding salt marsh outside sea wall	Salt marsh outside sea wall in 1688	Tenant and Term	Yearly rent	Amount of arable in 1688
Andes als Arundell Marsh Ridge als New-inned Marsh	nil	360a. of which 37a. described as 'wast' (Arundell 153a., Ridge 207a.)		Peter Porter from Michaelmas 1686 for 9 years	£180	138a.
Half of Eastwick Marsh	53a.	213a.	40a.	Peter Lodwick from Michaelmas 1686 for 15 years	£97 10s.	60a.
Other half of Eastwick Marsh	nil	161a.		Thomas Greeneway from Michaelmas 1686 for 15 years	£97 10s.	60a.
Foulness Hall als Old Hall and New Hall Marshes	nil	337a. of which 24a. described as 'wast'		Jesse Nauta and William Morebecke from Michaelmas 1686 for 21 years	£150	90a.
Old Lodge Marsh	nil	167a. of which 15a. described as 'wast'		Robert Bell from Michaelmas 1687 for 21 years	£78	50a.
Monken-barnes Marsh	65a.	218a.		Jonas Allen from Michaelmas 1686 for 19 years	£78	60a.
Naswick Marsh	51a.	420a.		Robert Bell from Michaelmas 1686 for 19 years	£150	5 or 6a.
New-house Marsh	53a.	250a. of which 21a. described as 'wast'	45a.	Robert Reeve from Michaelmas 1686 for 1 year	£80	70a.
Newick-Marsh	nil	221a. of which 15a. described as 'wast'	17a.	John Noble from Michaelmas 1687 for 12 years	£80	75a.
Priestwood-Marsh	37a.	275a.		John Lodwick from Michaelmas 1688 for 15 years	£120	90a.
Shelford Marsh	nil	545a.		Mr. Scrimshire on an annual basis	£260	100a.

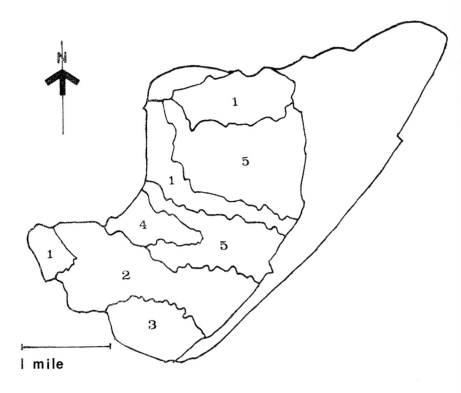

MAP 1

PRE-REFORMATION PARISH BOUNDARIES

1. Rochford.
2. Shopland.
3. Little Wakering and Shopland. It has not proved possible to define the boundary.
4. Little Stambridge.
5. Sutton.

The remainder is 'inned' land. New Wick, already 'inned' by *c*.1420 and Arundel Marsh, 'inned' 1424–86, remained extra-parochial until Foulness became a separate ecclesiastical parish. Later 'innings' automatically became part of Foulness Parish.

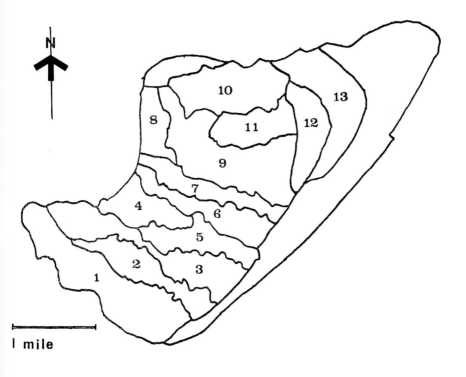

MAP 2

MEDIEVAL MARSHES AND WICKS

1. Shelford Marsh.
2. Little Burwood Marsh.
3. Great Burwood Marsh.
4. Clement Marsh.
5. New Marsh.
6. Rugwood Marsh.
7. Priestwood Marsh.
8. Monkton Barns Marsh.
9. South Wick (Foulness Hall).
10. Nase Wick.
11. East Wick.
12. New Wick ('inned' by *c*.1420).
13. Arundel Marsh ('inned' 1424–1486).

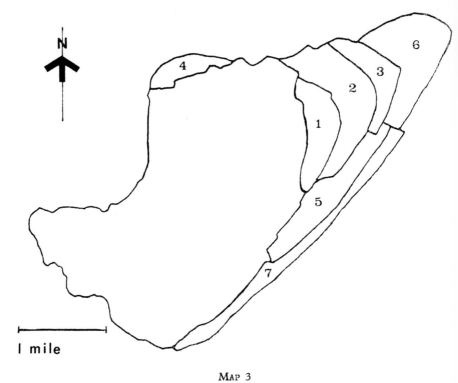

I mile

MAP 3

'INNINGS'

1. New Wick, by *c*.1420.
2. Arundel Marsh, 1424–1486.
3. Ridge Marsh, 1620–1662.
4. 1687–1688. Shared among adjoining farms of Nase Wick and Monkton Barns.
5. 1687–1688. Shared among adjoining farms of Rugwood, Priestwood, East Wick and New House.
6. East and West Newlands, 1801.
7. 1833. Shared among eight adjoining farms of West Newlands, Tree, East Wick, Rugwood, New Marsh, Great and Little Burwood, and Great Shelford.

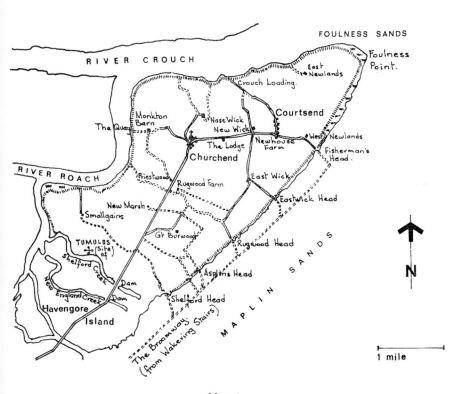

FOULNESS SANDS

RIVER CROUCH

Foulness
Point.

East
Newlands

Crouch Loading.

Monkton
Barn

The Quay

NaseWick
New Wick

Courtsend

West Newlands

The Lodge

Newhouse
Farm

Fisherman's
Head.

Churchend

RIVER ROACH

Priestwood

Rugwood Farm

East Wick

New Marsh

Eastwick Head

Smallgains

TUMULUS
(Site
of)

Gt Burwood

Rugwood Head

Shelford Creek

Asplins Head

M A P L I N   S A N D S

New England Creek

Dam

Dam

Shelford Head

Havengore

Island

The Broomway
(from Wakering Stairs)

N

1 mile

MAP 4

FOULNESS IN 1970

FOOTNOTES. All MSS. are in the Essex Record Office.

CHAPTER I
1. Much of the information in this chapter has been drawn from Chapter I of Miss Hilda Grieve's *The Great Tide* (1959). Reference has also been made to Gordon J. Copley, *An Archaeology of South-East England* (1958).
2. Chips of hard stone (usually flint, as at Clacton) used for cutting implements.
3. *Victoria County History of Essex* (V.C.H.), iii (Roman Gazetteer), 132.
4. *Ibid.*
5. *V.C.H.*, iii, 14.
6. *V.C.H.*, ii, 445.
7. Philip Benton, *History of the Rochford Hundred*, i, (1867), 176.
8. Edgar Brown, 'An Essex Island Parish', *Essex Review*, xxxvi (1927), 167.
9. Brown, 164.
10. P. H. Reaney, *Place-Names of Essex* (1935).

CHAPTER II
1. See below, p. 23 and Map 1.
2. *V.C.H.*, i, 369.
3. They were North and South Benfleet, Bowers Gifford, Hadleigh, Laindon, Pitsea, Prittlewell, Southchurch and Vange. See *V.C.H.*, i, 369.
4. For further details see J. Horace Round's 'Introduction to the Essex Domesday', *V.C.H.*, i, 333–426.
5. *Cal. Pat. Rolls*, 19 Hen. III.
6. Bailiff's accounts *c.* 1420 (D/DHt M45) and 1424 (D/DK M135).
7. See below, p. 29.
8. It was not in the hands of the de Bohun family in 1483 (*Cal. Pat. Rolls*, 22–3 Edw. IV) but appears in the Foulness bailiff's account, 1486 (D/DK M136). It is not mentioned in the two earlier accounts of *c.*1420 and 1424.
9. See below, p. 29. First mentioned in bailiff's account roll 1486 (D/DK M136).
10. See Maps 1 and 2. The 'inned' marshes remained extra-parochial until Foulness became a separate ecclesiastical parish in 1547 or 1549. See below, p. 23.
11. Philip Morant, *History of Essex*, i (1768), 324.
12. *Dictionary of National Biography*, *sub.* Hubert.
13. *Feet of Fines for Essex*, i, 275 (ed. R.E.G. Kirk, 1899–1910) and *Cal. Charter Rolls*, 17 Edw. II.
14. *Cal. Inq.*, 2 Edw. I.
15. *Cal. Close Rolls*, 2 Edw. I.
16. *Cal. Inq.*, 3 Edw. II.
17. *Cal. Charter Rolls* 17 Edw. II.
18. Morant, i, 324.
19. See below.
20. *Complete Peerage*, vi, 473–7.
21. Morant, i, 324.
22. *Complete Peerage*, vi, 474; *Cal. Close Rolls*, 9 Rich. II; *Cal. Pat. Rolls*, 8 Hen. IV. Lady Joan had assignment of dower on 26 July 1373.
23. Eleanor married Thomas of Woodstock (youngest son of Edw. III) and died in 1399 (*Complete Peerage*, vi, 474–5). Mary married Henry of Lancaster (who succeeded to the throne on 30 September 1399 as Henry IV) and died in 1394 (*Complete Peerage*, vi, 475).
24. *Complete Peerage*, vi, 474.
25. D/DK M136.
26. *Cal. Pat. Rolls*, 2 Rich. III.
27. *D.N.B.*, *sub.* James Butler.
28. *D.N.B.*, *sub.* James Butler and *Cal. Pat. Rolls*, 2 Rich. III. John and Thomas were pardoned by Edward IV shortly afterwards, and all the estates were restored, except those parts in Essex which had been granted to Edward's sister Anne in 1465.
29. *Cal. Pat. Rolls*, 5 Edw. IV.
30. *Cal. Pat. Rolls*, 12 Edw. IV and *D.N.B. sub.* Thomas Grey whose mother was Elizabeth Woodville who firstly married John Grey, 8th Baron Ferrers of Groby, and after his death at the battle of St. Albans (Feb. 1461) privately married Edward IV in 1464. Elizabeth had two sons by John Grey, Thomas and Richard.
31. *Cal. Pat. Rolls*, 2 Rich. III.
32. *D.N.B.*, *sub.* John Grey, 8th Baron Ferrers of Groby, and *Cal. Pat. Rolls*, 2 Rich. III.
33. *Cal. Pat. Rolls*, 2 Rich. III.
34. *D.N.B.*, *sub.* Thomas Boleyn whose mother was the daughter and co-heiress of Thomas Butler, 7th Earl of Ormond. The possession of the Ormond title had been in dispute for several years. In compensation Piers Butler was made Earl of Ossory in February 1528.
35. *D.N.B.*, *sub.* Thomas Boleyn.

36. *D.N.B.*, *sub*. Henry Carey. Mary's second husband was Sir William Stafford who died in 1543.
37. D/DA T623.
38. *V.C.H.*, i, 372.
39. D/DP M559.
40. See K. C. Newton, *The Manor of Writtle*, (1970), 68–85.
41. For an explanation of this term, see below.
42. *Walter of Henley's Husbandry*, ed. E. Lamond (Royal Hist. Soc., 1890).
43. See Map 2.
44. John Norden's MS. 'Description of Essex', 1594 (D/DMs P1).
45. *Pipe Rolls*, 19 Hen. II.
46. F. W. Steer, *Farm and Cottage Inventories of Mid Essex, 1633–1749* (1950), 37.
47. South Wick had probably ceased to be known as such by the mid-seventeenth century. In 1620 it was referred to as 'Southwick *alias* Foulness Hall' (D/DU 514/29/21) but by 1662 it was known only as the farm of Foulness Hall (D/DU 514/29/34).
48. Walter of Henley was a Dominican friar whose 'Hosebondrie', written about 1250, remained the best treatise on the subject until Fitzherbert's *Boke of Husbandrie* appeared in 1525 (*D.N.B.*).
49. Draught animals, probably oxen.
50. See above, p. 9 and Map 2.
51. See below, p. 23.
52. See below, p. 14.
53. See below, pp. 25–28.
54. Thomas Wright's *History of Essex*, ii (1836), 634.
55. See below p. 20.

CHAPTER III
1. D/DU 514/29/25.
2. D/DU 514/29/27.
3. D/DU 514/29/25b.
4. D/DA T623. Henry Carey was 1st Lord Hunsdon. See above, p. 10.
5. D/DU 514/29/17.
6. See below.
7. John Norden's MS. Description of Essex, 1594 (D/DMs P1).
8. William Camden's *Britannia*, last edn., 1607.
9. Daniel Finch (1647–1730), Tory statesman; eldest son of Heneage Finch, 1st Earl of Nottingham; succeeded to Earldom of Winchilsea, 9 Sept. 1729. See *D.N.B* for details.
10. See below, p. 21.
11. D/DK E1.
12. For the five farms see below, p. 29. For an explanation of the term 'inned' see below, p. 28.
13. D/DK E1.
14. William Harrison's *Description of England* (1577–87).
15. *The Agrarian History of England and Wales*, iv, 53–4, ed. Joan Thirsk (1967).
16. D/DK E1.
17. With the exception of the mention of mustard such clauses could apply to any marshland estate in Essex; they are not unique to Foulness.
18. A. F. J. Brown, *Essex at Work, 1700–1815* (1969), 39.
19. C. Shrimpton, 'The Landed Society and the Farming Community of Essex in the Late Eighteenth and Early Nineteenth Centuries', unpublished Ph. D. thesis (1961) in E.R.O. Library.
20. A. F. J. Brown, 35.
21. *Ibid*.
22. A reference to the Broomway. For details of this ancient track see below, p. 41.
23. Nath. Salmon's *History of Essex* (1740–42), 392.
24. D/DSf T19.
25. Shrimpton, 249.
26. Griggs' *General view of the Agriculture of the County of Essex* (1794), 12.
27. No doubt a reference to the floods of February 1736. See below, p. 31.
29. Young, i, 15.
29. Young, i, 18.
30. Young, ii, 122.
31. Young, i, 68
32. Shrimpton, 249.
33. Young, ii, 101.
34. Young, in turn, based his tables on Charles Vancouver's *Report to the Board of Agriculture on Essex* (1795).
35. Mustard had been grown on Foulness from 1424 (see p. 13). It is strange, therefore, that it should be regarded as 'unusuall' in 1688.
36. Vancouver.

37. Young, ii, 64.
38. *Ibid.*, 234.
39. *Ibid.*, 305.
39. *Ibid.*, 305.
40. *Ibid.*, 33.
41. See above, p. 18.
42. See above, p. 17.
43. Young, i, 221–2.
44. *Ibid.*, 373.
45. See above, p. 16.
46. Norden.
47. Daniel Defoe, *A Tour Through the Eastern Counties* (1722).
48. Young, i, 69.
49. See above, p. 16.
50. W. H. Dalton, 'Wells on Foulness Island, Ancient and Modern', *Essex Naturalist*, xv, (1907–8), 118–25.
51. Wright, ii, 634–6.
52. *Ibid.*, 636.
53. W. H. Dalton, 'Fowlness', *Ess. Nat.*, iii, 239–43.
54. D/CT 143.
55. See below, p. 29.
56. The tithe award schedule does not distinguish between arable and pasture in the case of New Marsh Farm. It has been estimated for the purposes of these calculations that 78 per cent (188 acres) was arable, and the remainder (63 acres) pasture.
57. *Post Office Directory*, 1870.
58. D/DSf T19.. It is probable that the bad flooding of 1897, which affected the southern part of Great Burwood Farm ('inned' land) also helped to depress the land value. See below, p. 31.
59. *Post Office Directory*, 1855.
60. D/DU 514/28.
61. *Ex inf.* Mr. and Mrs. P. A. Arnold, Lodge Farm, Foulness.

CHAPTER IV

1. D/CT 143 and D/DK E1.
2. See above, p. 9 and Map 1.
3. *Cal. Close Rolls*, 10 Rich. II, and Morant, ii, 324.
4. Newcourt's *Repertorium*, ii (1710), 271.
5. *Cal. Pat. Rolls*, 8 Hen. IV.
6. Newcourt, ii, 272–3. The tithes payable were presumably vicarial.
7. E. Brown, *Ess. Rev.*, xxxvi, 170. A sketch of this church, 1848, is reproduced in *Ess. Rev.* opp. p. 172.
8. See Map 1.
9. Benton, i, f.n., p. 182.
10. *Ibid.*
11. D/CT 143.
12. D/P 76/1/3.
13. *Ibid.*
14. E. Brown, *Ess. Rev.*, xxxvi, 179–80.
15. Benton, i, 207.
16. *Ibid.*, 207–8.
17. *Ibid.*, 208.
18. *Ibid.*, 210.
19. *Ibid.*

CHAPTER V

1. See above, p. 7.
2. See above, pp. 7, 8.
3. D/DEl M228.
4. D/DC 2/11–16; D/DGe M200, 201; D/DEl M214–29.
5. H. A. Blencowe, *The Story of the Garrison, Shoeburyness* (1945).
6. *Cal. Charter Rolls*, 17 Edw. II.
7. *Cal. Inq.*, 22 Edw. III.
8. D/DHt M45.
9. See Knight's *Practical Dictionary of Mechanics* (1874–77) for a full explanation.
10. D/DK M135.
11. D/DQs 189.
12. See Map 2.
13. T/A 262/4, 5.
14. Harrison.

15. Camden, 441. Canvey was finally walled early in the 1620s under the direction of the famous Dutch engineer Cornelius Vermuyden. See D. W. Gramolt 'The Coastal Marshlands of East Essex' (unpublished M.A. thesis (1960) in E.R.O.), 141.
16. 23 Hen. VIII c.5. Made permanent in 1549 by 3 and 4 Edw. VI c.8.
17. This is all based on the MS. case for counsel's opinion drawn up by the islanders, with comments inserted by Brodrick (D/DU 514/33).
18. The Keeper of the Great Seal.
19. The outcome is unknown.
20. D/SN 1.
21. See above, p. 26.
22. See Map 1.
23. See above, p. 23.
24. The earliest reference to Arundel Marsh is in the bailiff's account roll for 1486 (D/DK M136.) It has not been possible to assign a more definite date to this 'inning' because of the gap in the account rolls between 1424 and 1486.
25. See her *The Great Tide* (1959), 14–21.
26. D/DU 514/28/34.
27. Except Shelford which is also 'marsh'.
28. D/DU 514/29/21.
29. D/DK E1. See Map 3.
30. See above, p. 16.
31. A new farm carved out of Arundel Marsh sometime before 1620, the date it is first mentioned (D/DU 514/29/33). No mention of it appears in the terrier of 1577 (D/DU 514/29/17).
32. D/DK E1. For areas of the 'innings' of 1687–88 see Map 3.
33. Young, ii, 255.
34. D/DSf T19. See Map 3.
35. See above, p. 7.
36. See above, p. 25.
37. See above, p. 25.
38. Matt. Paris, *Rolls Series*, p. 379.
39. Grieve, 12.
40. D/DHf T90.
41. Brown, 169–70.
42. Stow's *Memorandum*, 129.
43. Camden Soc. N.S., xxviii.
44. Holinshed's *Chronicle*.
45. Camden, 441.
46. Pepys' *Diary*, The whole of Whitehall was under water.
47. D/DU 514/33. See above, p. 27.
48. Salmon, 426.
49. *The Gentleman's Magazine*, Feb. 1736.
50. See above, p. 28.
51. Grieve, 44–5.
52. D/SN 3.
53. *Ess. Nat.*, xv, 52.
54. *Ibid.*
55. Grieve, 53.

CHAPTER VI
1. This chapter is based wholly on extracts from Miss Grieve's *The Great Tide* (1959).

CHAPTER VII
1. See above, p. 20.
2. See above, p. 20.
3. The family of Cripps is still on the island. The wills of James Cripes, husbandman, 1596, John Crypes, 1581, John Cripes, sen., 1586, John Cryppes, 1587, William Crips, 1581, William Cripes, fisherman, 1604, all of Foulness, are preserved in the E.R.O. See *Wills at Chelmsford*, i (1440–1619), ed. F. G. Emmison (1958).
4. Benton, i, 214.
5. See below, pp. 39, 40.
6. Benton, i, 214.
7. Q/SBb 248/41, 286/12, 29, 287/21.
8. The churchyard adjoins the 'George and Dragon'. At the time 'no fence existed between it and the grounds of the public house' (Benton, i, 214).
9. Benton, i, 216.
10. See above, p. 20.
11. Benton, i, 225.
12. Benton, i, 214. There is still no resident policeman on the island.
13. Benton, i, 210.
14. Two-thirds of the island belonged to that family until 1915.

15. Benton, i, 181–2.
16. E. Brown, *Ess. Rev.*, xxxvi, 178.
17. Benton, i, 213–4.
18. See above, pp. 13, 14.
19. An examination of the wills of person bearing the same surnames as those engaged in the fishing industry has indicated that the fishermen were resident in the neighbouring mainland parishes. See *Wills at Chelmsford*, i.
20. See above, p. 17.
21. See below, p. 42.
22. See above, p. 29.
23. From about 1921 the census includes a number of servicemen and their families, resident on the island. The 'native' population has therefore fallen faster in the twentieth century than the table indicates, to a present day level of about 150.
24. Described as 'private households'.
25. See above, p. 20.
26. Until the 19th century they appear to have been landless labourers.
27. *Ex inf.* Mr. P. A. Arnold who conducted the survey and who, with his wife, has analysed the parish registers.
28. By our standards, though not exceptional for the period.
29. See above, p. 20.
30. Benton, i, 226.
31. D/P 76/1/2.
32. Young, ii, 389.
33. Benton, i, 226.
34. D/P 76.
35. Benton, i, 178.
36. See above, p. 14.
37. A. F. J. Brown, 88.
38. See above, p. 24.
39. The Rectory was built at the expense of the patron of the living and lord of the manor, George Finch, replacing an earlier building (E. Brown, *Ess. Rev.*, xxxvi, 179).
40. Benton, i, 188.
41. D/P 76/1/2. See note in *Essex Parish Records*, ed. F. G. Emmison (1966), 119.
42. E. Brown, *Ess. Rev.*, xxxvi, 184.
43. *Ibid.*, 183.
44. See above, p. 29.
45. D/P 76/1/1–3.
46. All information concerning wildfowl has been extracted from R. Hudson and G. A. Pyman, *A Guide to the Birds of Essex* (1968).

CHAPTER VIII
1. Q/RUm 2/80.
2. 15–16 Vict. c.lxvi. See also D/DMb O3.
3. 29–30 Vict. c.lxix.
4. Edgar Brown, *History of Bradwell-on-Sea*, 148.
5. T/A 453 (microfilm of papers preserved in House of Lords R.O.).
6. Q/RUm 2/143.
7. D. W. Gramolt, 'The Coastal Marshlands of East Essex' (unpublished M.A. thesis (1960) in E.R.O.), 113.

INDEX

Gifford, Richard, Bishop of London: 23
Gloucester, Richard, Duke of: 10
Great Lodge: 23. *See also* Lodge Farm
Greeneway, Thomas: 49
Grey: Richard, Lord, 10; Thomas, Marquis of Dorset, 10

Ham, West, marshes: 25
Hambley, William: 24
Hammond, William, shepherd of Newyk: 12
Harrison: John, Thomas, 15
Harrys, William: 15
Havengore Island: 8
'Headways': 41
Holliwell Point: 44
Horse Pastures: 13, 14
Housing. *See* Statistics

Ice Ages: 7, 25

Jaywick, Lion Point: 7
Justice: Richard, Robert, 15

Kennitt, Edward, yeoman: 18
Kiddells (kiddles): 13, 14, 20–22, 41
Knapping, John: 29
Kynge, John, of Burnham, fisherman: 14

Land Drainage Act (1930): 25
Langenhoe, manor and marshes: 25
Laurence, Samuel: 38
Lawson: Robert, widow of William: 15
Lifeboat, Southend: 34
Liverpool Observation and Tidal Institute: 30
Livestock. *See* Carthorses; Cattle; Sheep
Lodge Farm: 23, 42. *See also* Great Lodge
Lodwick: John, 17, 49; Peter, 49

Maplin Sands: 20, 21, 41, 44
Metropolis Sewage and Essex Reclamation Company: 44
Mission Hall: 20, 42
Monkton Barns: farm, 35; marsh, 9, 11, 13, 26, 29, 49
Morebecke, William: 49

Nase (Naze) Wick: 9, 11–13, 16, 17, 26, 29, 49
Nauta, Jesse: 49
New England Island: 8
New Hall Marsh: 49. *See also* Foulness Hall; Old Hall
New House: farm, 20, 21, 34, 41; marsh, 29, 49
New Marsh: 15, 26
New Wick: 9, 11–13, 16, 26, 29, 31, 49
Newlands, East and West: 29, 49
Noble, John: 49
Nott: James, Richard, 17

Old Hall: marsh, 49. *See also* Foulness Hall; South Wick
Old Lodge Marsh: 23, 49. *See also* Lodge Farm.
'Othona', Roman fort: 8

Paglesham: 9
Parish: cage, 42; registers, 42
Parishes, detached parts: Canvey Island, 9; Foulness, 9, 23, 24; Wallasea Island, 9. *See also* Map 1
Peek: family, fishermen, 14; Ralph son of John, 26
Place-name evidence: 8
Police: 38
Poor house: 42
Population. *See* Statistics
Porter, Peter: 16, 49
Potton Island: 8, 41
Powley, Rev. Sidney: 24
Priestwood: farm, 20, 35, 42; marsh, 16, 26, 29, 49
Produce: barley, 20, 22; beans, 13, 20, 22; beef, 20; butter, 10, 16, 17; cheese, 12, 17, 26; fleeces, 12; milk of ewes, 11; milk of calves and cows, 12; mustard, 13, 17, 19, 20, 22; mutton, 20; oats, 13, 22; peas, 20; sheepskins, 12; wheat, 13, 20, 22; wool, 12, 21
Public houses: 'George and Dragon', 38, 42; 'King's Head', 39

Raim, John: 17
Rawlyn: Edward, Thomas, 15
Ray Sand: 44
Reclamation. *See* Metropolis Sewage and Essex Reclamation Company; South Essex Estuary and Reclamation Company
Rectories: 20
Rede, John, shepherd of Nassewyk: 12
Red Hills: 8
Reeve, Robert: 49
Rennie, Sir John: 44
Rents: 15–19, 49
Rich: family, 16; Charles, 4th Earl of Warwick, 16, 29; Lady Essex, 16; Mary, widow of 4th Earl, 16; Sir Richard, Lord Chancellor, 10, 15; Robert, 29
Ridge Marsh: 16, 29, 42, 49
Roach, River: 28, 41
Roads: military road from Great Wakering, 34, 35, 41, 44; state of, 41. *See also* Broomway
Rochford: 9, 23, 50
Rochford: Sir Guy de, 9, 10; Margery, widow of Guy de, Robert de, 10
Rochford Hundred: 12, 16, 20, 23, 25, 41
Rugwood: farm, 20, 33, 35, 36, 42; Head, 33; marsh, 9, 26, 29; mound at, 8
Rushley Island: 8, 20

St. Osyth's Priory: 12
St. Peter's Sands: 44
Sales Point: 44
Saltings: 28, 29
Salt works: 8
Schools: 20, 38, 41, 42
Scrimshire, Mr: 49
Sea-walls: 26
Sewers: Commission(er)s of, 27, 31; act of 1532, 27. *See also* Commissions of Walls and Ditches; Land Drainage Act
Sheep: 11–13; breeds, 19, 20; sickness, 11. *See also* Produce